QIANJIADU
钱 家 渡

王建国　朱　渊　宗袁月　著

东南大学出版社
南京

内容简介

近年来，在国家持续实施"乡村振兴战略"的大背景下，我国对"三农"问题的关注和乡村建设日益升温。随着中央一系列政策和地方实践的推进，乡村建设正走向在地化、特色化和可持续化道路。

本书中的钱家渡村乡村建设是"江苏省特色田园乡村建设"行动的组成部分。本书详细记述了南京江宁钱家渡村2017—2020年的建设历程，在上位规划的语境下着重论述并呈现了钱家渡乡村建设实践的缘起、过程、构思设计和实施成果，结合乡村公共空间和人居环境的优化，探索了中国有特色的在地性乡村振兴的可行之路。

本书可供乡村建设相关从业者、建筑师、规划师、乡村问题研究者，以及社会公众阅读参考。

图书在版编目（CIP）数据

钱家渡 / 王建国，朱渊，宗袁月著. —南京：
东南大学出版社，2020.12
 ISBN 978-7-5641-9329-4

Ⅰ.①钱… Ⅱ.①王… ②朱… ③宗… Ⅲ.①农村－社会主义建设－研究－南京 Ⅳ.① F327.531

中国版本图书馆 CIP 数据核字（2020）第 257704 号

钱家渡
QIANJIADU

著　　者：王建国　朱　渊　宗袁月
责任编辑：戴　丽
责任印刷：周荣虎

出版发行：东南大学出版社
社　　址：南京市四牌楼 2 号
邮　　编：210096
网　　址：http://www.seupress.com
出 版 人：江建中

印　　刷：上海雅昌艺术印刷有限公司
开　　本：889 mm × 1194 mm　　1/20　印张：9　字数：200 千字
版 印 次：2020 年 12 月第 1 版　2020 年 12 月第 1 次印刷
书　　号：ISBN 978-7-5641-9329-4
定　　价：88.00 元

经　　销：全国各地新华书店
发行热线：025-83790519　83791830

* 版权所有，侵权必究
* 本社图书若有印装质量问题，请直接与营销部联系。电话：025-83791830

钱家渡

前言　FOREWORD

英国诗人库伯曾经说："上帝创造了乡村，人类创造了城市。"中国社会学家费孝通经过多年的研究，认为"乡村蕴含着中国社会经济变迁中的一切基因"。

世界各地的乡村聚落林林总总，无一不与特定的地域气候条件、地形地貌、聚落生活方式和乡土文化传统息息相关。乡村民居建筑及其乡村环境的营造大多采用的是民间"自下而上"的组织方法。它们按照"顺应自然"或"经济实用"的方式，遵循有机体的生长原则，依靠共同的语言和传统维系。通常，乡村建筑环境风貌的整体价值要高于单体价值。绝大多数的乡村居民主要基于自身需要和价值取向建设了各自的聚落人居环境，而这种建设活动主要是依靠地方工匠和乡民所为。

中国自古"以农立国"。山清水秀，"小桥流水人家"，一直是乡村画境般的存在，农耕聚落是中华民族发展历史和五千年华夏文明的重要见证和载体。多少年来，由就地取材、世代相传方式运作的工匠建造方式，以特定社区生活圈，如以姓氏祠堂为中心的社会组织形式为基础的生活和审美习性，造就了华夏大地上"五里不同俗，十里不同风"的乡村地域和建筑风貌的丰富多彩。然而，在近半个世纪里，在"重工轻农"的发展政策导向下，城乡二元对立、歧视性的户籍制等造成了广大农村建设相比城市要严重滞后，乡村建筑风貌每况愈下，文化传承出现危机。

党的十九大首次提出"乡村振兴战略"，并将其作为贯彻新发展理念，建设现代化经济体系的重要举措之一。《乡村振兴战略规划（2018—2022年）》明确提出从不同村庄的特点、资源和区位出发，分类推进乡村发展，并首次确定了集聚提升类、特色保护类、城郊融合类、搬迁撤并类等四类村庄的差异化发展定位。其中，"城郊融合类"主要是指城市近郊村这类具有特殊区位属性的乡村，其面临的机遇和挑战与传统意义上的农村差异巨大。

钱家渡村位于秦淮河、溧水河、句容南河交汇处，从区位上讲属城市近郊村。钱家渡村至今保持着原生态的江南水乡风貌，基地内部水网密布、塘田交错，然而资源种类及景观资源单体较少，较为普通贫乏。2017年，钱家渡村入选江苏省特色田园乡村建设首批试点村庄，开始了新的发展振兴进程，但此时大部分农户已经另易其业。根据钱家渡村当地圩区水系发达的特点，南京市、江宁区政府部署确立在钱家渡打造以水乡田园为主题的特色田园乡村，综合近郊旅游、乡村服务及体验功能。

2017年，我们有幸应邀参加了钱家渡村改造和环境提升的技术工作，在前期南京城理人城市规划设计团队的策划和概念规划基础上，根据原有村民宅基地不变以及原有小学和水利泵站建筑用地功能置换的原则，团队先后开展并完成了游客中心、民宿、书屋、清吧、水上餐厅和相关的景观设计提升。团队编制了村民住宅改造的"菜单式"技术图则，指导并鼓励他们按照各自喜好的菜单图样自行改造住房。经过2年左右的时间，团队先后完成村庄房屋外立面改造53栋，适当提高房屋屋顶，增加玻璃和木质结构，提高了房屋的透光性和舒适度；开展水系梳理3.8公里，打造水上交通游线；增设了便民服务点、公共厕所和垃圾分类设施。目前村庄的环境整治、基础设施、旅游配套设施等项目的建设工作基本完成，村容、村貌大为改善，并于2019年"五一"假期对外试运营，吸引了5万多名游客慕名而来。同时，不少乡民返乡创业，钱家渡村停车场旁的和平饭店，就是景区内第一家村民经营的农家乐。

钱家渡村的建筑改造和设计分成了几种类型。首先大部分公共建筑在原民宅基础上进行改造，而特定节点建筑出于功能的要求，采用相对集中的布局方式。滨水民宿改造保留了原始布局，而水上餐厅和清吧则通过重塑场地肌理延续村庄集体记忆。

乡村书屋建在存量闲置的宅基地上，由于是集体建设用地，可以进行自然村公共及公益事业项目的改造出新及新建。书屋设计强化了传统空间氛围和属性，采用了稍具异质特征的空间组织和设计手法，适应了村民新的文化需求，现在已经是农村基层组织活动的中心场所。在乡村生活馆的设计中，传统材料的全新利用方式展现出乡土材料和建造方式的更新，而民宿中心则是尝试采用工业材料转译乡村形态。

经历了钱家渡村的乡村振兴策略的实施和建设过程，我们的体会是，乡村建设一定要能够静得下心、沉得住气、贴近真实在地的乡村振兴诉求，多关注"过程导向"而非简单的"项目导向"和"技术下乡"。同时要关注基于村民自觉、自愿、自为的推动力，弥补标准化、单纯的速度和市场导向的发展模式缺陷。事实上，我们不可能完成所有的村民所需要的民宅提升和改造诉求，而技术图则恰恰可以充当我们设计转译和技术指导的"二传手"。

钱家渡村改造基本完成后，受到了各方面的好评，市场热度和关注度持续提升。不少领导和我讲起，说钱家渡村做得很成功，但我清醒地知道，一个村民喜闻乐见的优秀环境的成长和成熟还需要时间的磨砺，钱家渡村的工程实践在造价、工期、施工精度、材料选择等方面还存在不少缺憾，期待总结经验，日后再有乡村建设机会时改进提升。

最后，必须要感谢在钱家渡村特色田园乡村项目策划、规划设计和建造过程中做出贡献的江宁区委区政府、南京市规划和自然资源局江宁分局、江宁旅游产业集团、南京城理人城市规划设计有限公司等。

2020年10月

Cooper, the English poet once said, "God made the country, and man made the town." Chinese sociologist Fei Xiaotong, after years of research, believes that "the countryside contains all the genes of China's socio-economic changes".

There are many rural settlements around the world, all of which are closely related to specific regional climatic conditions, topography, settlement lifestyles and vernacular cultural traditions. Most of the rural residential buildings and the surrounding environment are created by traditional "bottom-up" organization method, Following the principles of organic growth and relying on common language and traditions in accordance with the "natural" or "economic and practical" approach. Usually, the overall value of the rural built environment is higher than the value of individual unit. The majority of rural residents have built their habitat basing on their own needs and value orientation, and this kind of construction activity mainly depends on local craftsmen and villagers.

Since ancient times, China has been "a country of agriculture". The beautiful natural sceneries along with small bridges and flowing water have always existed in the picturesque countryside, and the farming settlements are important witness and carrier of the history of Chinese nation along with 5,000-year-long Chinese civilization. For many years, the artisan construction method, which is based on local materials and passed down from generation to generation, and the living and aesthetic habits resulted from specific community life circles, such as the social organization form centering on the ancestral hall for the family name, have created a rich and colorful rural area and architectural style of "different customs from five miles away and different styles from ten miles away" on the land of China. However, in the past half century, under the development policy of "lay stress on industry at the expense of agriculture", the dichotomy between urban and rural areas and the discriminatory household registration system have caused a serious lag in the construction of the vast rural areas, comparing to the cities, which resulted in the deterioration of rural architecture and the crisis in cultural inheritance.

The 19th CPC National Congress put forward the "rural revitalization strategy" for the first time, making it one of the important measures to implement the new development concept and build a modern economic system. The *National Rural Revitalization Strategic Plan (2018-2022)* clearly proposes to promote rural development in a categorized manner based on the characteristics, resources and location of different villages, and determines the differentiated development positioning for four types of villages, including the clustering and upgrading category, the characteristic protection category, the suburban integration category, and the relocation and removal category. Among them, "suburban integration category" mainly refers to villages with special location attributes such as suburban villages, which are facing huge differences in opportunities and challenges from the traditional rural areas.

Qianjiadu village is located at the confluence of Qinhuai River, Lishui River and Jurong South River, which is a suburban village in terms of location. The Village has maintained the original Jiangnan water village appearance so far, with a dense water network and staggered ponds and fields inside the base. However, there are fewer resource types and landscape resource alone. In 2017, Qianjiadu Village was selected as one of the first batch of pilot villages in Jiangsu Province for the construction of characteristic rural area, and started a new revitalization process. Nevertheless, most of the farmers have changed their businesses at this time. Based on the well-developed water system of the Village, Nanjing and Jiangning district governments deployed to establish a characteristic rural village with the theme of water countryside in Qianjiadu, which integrates suburban tourism, rural services and experience functions.

We were honored to be invited to participate in the technical work of the renovation and environmental enhancement of Qianjiadu Village in 2017. Based on the planning and conceptual planning by NanJing CITYAGENT Urban Planning Design Co. Ltd., with the principle of unchanging the original villagers' house bases and replacing the functions of the original elementary school and the building site of the water conservancy pumping station, our team has carried out and completed the design of the visitor center, the B&B, the book house, the bar, the water restaurant and the related landscape upgrading successively. With the designed "menu" of technical drawings for the villagers' housing renovation, the team guided and encouraged them to renovate their houses according to their preferred menu drawings. After about 2 years, in the village the team has completed the renovation of 53 houses' facades, raised the roofs of houses appropriately, added glass and wooden structures, improving the light permeability and living comfort; carried out 3.8-kilometer-long water system renewal project to create a water transportation line; installed additional convenient service points, public toilets and garbage sorting facilities. At present, the construction of environmental improvement, infrastructure, tourism facilities and other projects in the village is basically completed, and the village appearance has been greatly improved. The trial operation was held on May 1,2019, attracting more than 50,000 tourists. At the same time, many villagers returned to their hometown to start their own businesses. the Peace Restaurant, next to Qianjiadu village parking lot, is the first restaurant run by villagers.

The architectural renovation and design in Qianjiadu Village is divided into several types. Firstly most of the public buildings are reconstructed on the basis of the original residential buildings, while specific node buildings adopt a relatively concentrated layout for functional requirements. The waterside homestay renovation preserves the original layout, while the waterside restaurant and bar continue the collective memory of the village by reshaping the texture of the site.

The village reading room is built on the stock of unused house bases, and since the construction land is collective-owned, it can be transformed or newly built for public welfare projects in the natural village. The design of the reading room strengthens the traditional spatial atmosphere and attributes, adopting spatial organization and design techniques with slightly heterogeneous characteristics to adapt to the new cultural needs of villagers. Now it is a central place for the activities of rural grassroots organizations. In the design of village life hall, the new way of using traditional materials shows the renewal of vernacular materials and construction methods, while the Homestay Service Center is an attempt to use industrial materials to translate rural forms.

After the implementation and construction of the rural revitalization strategy for Qianjiadu Village, our experience is that rural construction must be done in a calm way, responding to the real local demands of rural revitalization with more attention to "process-oriented" rather than simple "project-oriented" and "technology to the countryside". At the same time, we have to mind the driving force based on villagers' consciousness, voluntariness and self-motivation, and make up for the shortcomings of the standardized, purely speedy and market-oriented development model. In fact, it is impossible for us to complete all the villagers' demands for upgrading and renovating their houses, so the technical drawings can serve as a "second hand" to translate our design and technical guidance.

After the transformation of Qianjiadu Village was basically completed, it was well received by all parties, with the market heat and attention continuing to rise. Many leaders talked to me about it, saying that Qianjiadu village did a very successful job, but I soberly know that the growth and maturity of an excellent environment that villagers like to see still needs time to sharpen, and the engineering practice of Qianjiadu village still has many shortcomings in terms of cost, construction period, construction precision, material selection, etc. I look forward to summing up the experience and improving and upgrading it later when there is another village construction opportunity.

Finally, thanks must be given to Jiangning People's District Government, Jiangning Branch of Nanjing Municipal Bureau of Planning and Natural Resources, the Jiangning Tourism Industry Group, and NanJing CITYAGENT Urban Planning Design Co. Ltd., who contributed to the planning,design and construction of the Qianjiadu Characteristic Rural Areas project.

2020.10

目录　INDEX

01	背景	Background	21
02	规划	Planning	29
03	建筑	Architecture	43
04	导则	Renovation Guideline	127
05	景观	Landscape	143
06	后续	Follow-up	165

01 背景
Background

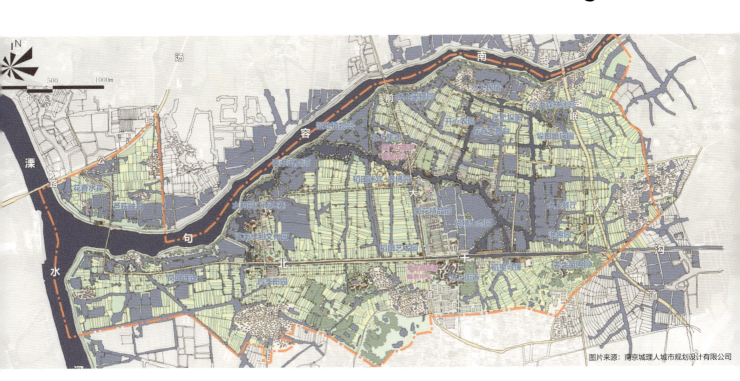

图片来源：南京城理人城市规划设计有限公司

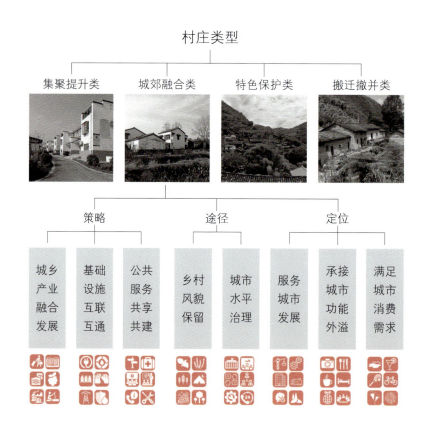

01 背景　Background

国家"乡村振兴战略"
National Rural Revitalization Strategy

2017 年 10 月 18 日，习近平同志在党的十九大报告中提出要实施乡村振兴战略。十九大报告指出，农业农村农民问题是关系国计民生的根本性问题，必须始终把解决好"三农"问题作为全党工作重中之重。要坚持农业农村优先发展，按照产业兴旺、生态宜居、乡风文明、治理有效、生活富裕的总要求，建立健全城乡融合发展体制机制和政策体系，加快推进农业农村现代化。

2018 年 1 月 2 日，国务院公布了 2018 年中央一号文件，即《中共中央国务院关于实施乡村振兴战略的意见》，明确了分阶段实现乡村振兴战略的目标任务。2018 年 9 月 26 日，中共中央、国务院印发《乡村振兴战略规划（2018—2022 年）》（以下简称《规划》）。自此，乡村振兴战略的内涵更为全面丰富。《规划》对实施乡村振兴战略做出阶段性谋划，并通过细化实化工作重点和政策措施，部署重大工程、重大计划、重大行动，确保战略的落实落地。

《规划》的第三篇第九章明确提出了"分类推进乡村发展"的策略，即：顺应村庄发展规律和演变趋势，根据不同村庄的发展现状、区位条件、资源禀赋等，按照集聚提升、融入城镇、特色保护、搬迁撤并的思路，分类推进乡村振兴，不搞一刀切。

On October 18, 2017, Comrade Xi Jinping proposed to implement the strategy of rural revitalization in the report of the 19th CPC National Congress. The report pointed out that the issue of agricultural and rural farmers is a fundamental issue related to the national economy and the people's livelihood, and that solving the "three rural" issues must always be the top priority of the Party's work.

On January 2, 2018, the State Council announced the No. 1 Central Document of 2018, which clarified the strategic objectives and tasks of rural revitalization to be achieved in stages. On September 26, 2018, the *National Rural Revitalization Strategic Plan (2018-2022)* (hereinafter referred to as the *Planning*) was issued. Since then, the connotation of the rural revitalization strategy has become more comprehensive and rich. The *Planning* makes a phased plan for the implementation of the rural revitalization strategy, and through detailed and actual work priorities and policy measures, plans and action are deployed to ensure the implementation of the strategy.

The *Planning* clearly proposes the revitalization strategy of "promoting rural development by classification". That is: in line with the nature and evolution of village development, according to the development status of different villages, location conditions, resource endowments, etc., the promotion of rural revitalization ought to be assessed and classified.

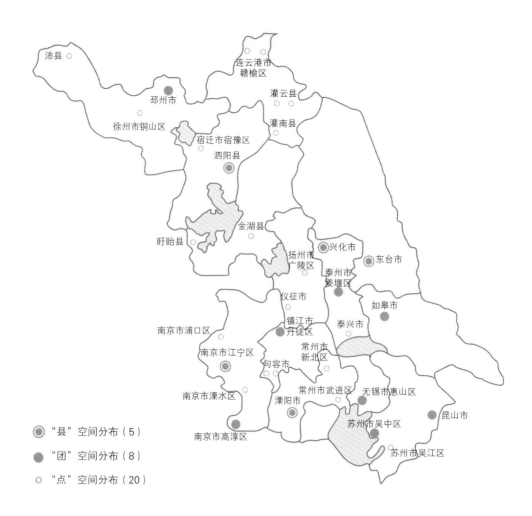

江苏省特色田园乡村
Characteristic Rural Areas in Jiangsu Province

2017年6月,江苏省委、省政府正式印发《江苏省特色田园乡村建设行动计划》,以"生态优、村庄美、产业特、农民富、集体强、乡风好"为总体目标实现乡村振兴。相比于"美丽乡村"建设,特色田园乡村建设不仅重视村庄环境,也强调村庄周边田园、山水环境的保育和提升;不仅致力于乡村旅游业的发展,也重点关注乡村特色产业发展以及产业的综合;不仅注重对乡村历史文物的保护,也深入挖掘转译乡土文化、乡贤文化和乡村本土性特色。特色田园乡村建设不是"美丽乡村"建设的延续,而是具有更加宏观和统筹性的视野,弥补早期乡村建设统筹不足带来的问题。

按照地方推荐、联合会商、地域统筹、涵盖多种农业产业类型、兼顾探索经济薄弱村脱贫等原则,首批省级特色田园乡村形成了"5县8团20个点"试点候选地区和村庄名单。南京市江宁区是入选首批试点村庄候选名单"5县"之一,开展5个田园特色乡村建设试点,侧重于县域的工作推进和机制创新振兴。

In June 2017, the Jiangsu Provincial Party Committee and the Provincial Government formally issued the *Province Characteristic Rural Areas Construction Action Plan in Jiangsu*, aiming to achieve the overall goal of "excellent ecology, beautiful villages, special industries, rich farmers, strong collectives, and good rural customs". The construction of characteristic rural areas not only pays attention to the village environment, but also emphasizes the preservation and improvement of the rural, landscape and environment surrounding the village. The action commits to the development of rural tourism as well as rural characteristic industries. Rural historical cultural relics are protected by digging into the translation of rural culture, rural sage culture and rural local characteristics. With a more macroscopic and overall perspective, the action aims to make up for the problems caused by the lack of overall planning of early rural construction.

In accordance with several principles, the first batch of provincial level characteristic rural villages formed the pilot candidate areas and villages of "5 counties, 8 groups and 20 spots" List. Jiangning District of Nanjing was selected as one of the "5 counties", and launched 5 rural village construction pilots, focusing on county work promotion and mechanism innovation and revitalization.

江宁区 从"美丽乡村"到"特色田园乡村"
From "Beautiful Village" to "Characteristic Rural Areas" in Jiangning District

"美丽乡村"一词在乡村建设中广泛运用,其概念最初在党的十六大上第一次明确提出,后由2013年中央一号文件正式阐述,其具体内容主要包含"生产发展、生活宽裕、乡风文明、村容整洁、管理民主"等要求。在各省市的推进落实中,"美丽乡村"建设包含了一系列具体的建设工作。

南京市江宁区"美丽乡村"建设是中央政策落地实践的缩影,也是江宁从工业开发园区导向的发展模式向城乡互动、多产业统筹发展模式逐渐转化的过程,从2011年开始至今,一共经历了四个阶段的发展。

具体来看,"美丽乡村"建设的第一阶段由政府主导,集中打造"五朵金花"美丽示范村,通过农家乐开发、整治、优化乡村风貌和空间,吸引城市人群;第二阶段以政府带动多元投资,"以点带面"扩大示范区域;第三阶段建立多元主体长效合作机制,拟定多层次的建设导则,以"千村整治、百村示范"计划覆盖70%的村庄;第四阶段以品质发展、功能弥合、特色塑造为主要内容,以"特色田园乡村"推动乡村从基础建设到特色文化培育,从单一旅游向乡村复合产业发展。

The term "beautiful village" is widely used in rural renovation projects. Its content mainly includes "production development, rich life, civilized rural style, clean environment, democratic management, etc.". In the implementation of various provinces and cities, the construction of "beautiful village" includes a series of specific construction work.

The construction of "beautiful villages" in Jiangning District, Nanjing is the epitome of the central government's policy implementation. It is also the process of the gradual transformation from an industry oriented development model to an urban rural interaction and multi industry coordinated development model. It has experienced four stages of development.

The first stage is led by the government, focusing on building "five golden flowers" as models, and optimizing the rural space through the development and renovation of farmhouses to attract urban people. The second stage focuses on driving mutiple investment, expands the demonstration area from "points to areas"; The third stage establishes a long-term cooperation mechanism with multiple subjects, and draws up multi level construction guideline. The fourth stage aims at qualified and featured development. The "characteristic rural area" is used to promote the development of rural areas from infrastructure construction to characteristic cultural cultivation, from single tourism to rural composite industries.

02 规划
Planning

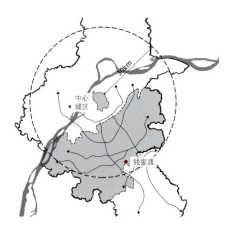

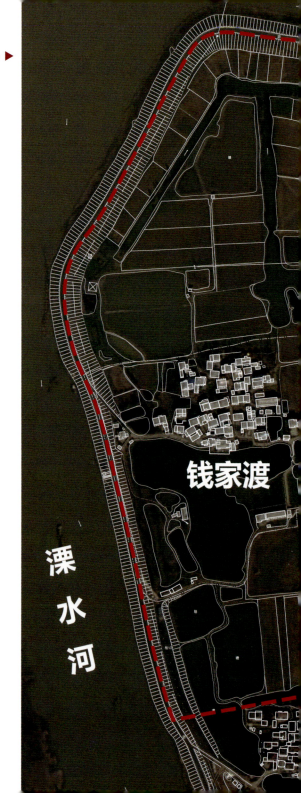

更新前村庄总平面　Past Master Plan ▶

村庄旧貌　Past of the Village

钱家渡村北临句容南河，西至溧水河，南接北干沟，为三面临水的圩区聚落。圩区内地形平坦，地势低洼，塘田交错。村域范围内生态环境良好，视野开阔，景观怡人。非建设用地以水田和浅塘为主，林地较少，水域整体水质较好。农田以养殖水面和稻田为主，田地沿主要水渠布置，肌理自然，体量较小，多为人工种植。

钱家渡村内多种时期建筑并存。以青砖、石块为主要材料的老旧民舍多建于20世纪60年代，为典型的江南水乡建筑，是村庄特色的重要体现，如今多处于荒置状态。现代民舍多建于20世纪80到90年代，以二层砖混结构为主，在形体和体量上相似，但立面和围墙的材料选择和色彩受城市建筑风格影响严重，与水乡田园特色风貌不协调。

钱家渡村现状主要通过西侧堤顶路进村，仅一处出入口，位于村庄西侧，进村道路坡度陡，便捷性和安全性较差，且村庄内部缺少停车空间。

Qianjiadu Village is bordered by Jurong South River, Lishui River and Beigan Ditch, being a polder area facing water on three sides. The polder area is flat, low-lying, with staggered ponds and fields. With excellent ecological environment, the non-construction land is dominated by paddy fields and shallow ponds. The farmland is dominated by aquaculture water surface.

The buildings of various periods coexist in Qianjiadu Village. Old houses with bricks and stones as the main materials were mostly built in the 1960s, becoming an important manifestation of village characteristics. Modern houses were mostly built in the 1980s and 1990s, mainly two story brick concrete structures which are similar in shape and volume. However, the choice of materials and colors for facades and walls is seriously affected by urban architectural styles.

Currently, the entrance of the village is located on the west side of the village. The entering road has a steep slope, leading to poor convenience and safety. There is a lack of parking space inside the village.

▲ 聚落鸟瞰 Birdview

02 规划 Planning

▲ 自然环境 Environment

▲ 建筑原貌 Architecture

▲ 道路设施 Infrastructure

规划总平面　Master Plan ▶

乡村新颜　Present of the Village

▲ 功能分区　Function Division
图片由南京城理人城市规划设计有限公司提供

▲ 交通组织　Transportation Orgnization

▲ 水系梳理　Water System
图片由南京城理人城市规划设计有限公司提供

设计立足乡村社会，融合现代文明，通过分别应对水域生态空间、田园生产空间、民居生活空间的风貌改造策略，营造富有地域特色且承载田园乡愁的村庄空间。

首先，通过提升村庄农业生产功能，实现传统生产空间与景观空间的复合。其中，在一般旱田、大面积水田打造田园景观，在村边、村庄内部菜地开展农事体验活动，希望通过功能叠合实现乡村生产空间的城乡共享。

其次，满足原住民和城市居民的生活需求，在乡村风貌形态下置入城市水平服务功能。其中包括，针对村民集会和文化需求，增加村民书屋，为村民提供阅读、上网、集会服务兼顾游客茶歇、会议需求；提取江南水乡"滨水而居"的传统生活方式，新增滨水民宿群及民宿服务中心，特色化居住带给游客悠然水乡的生活体验；回应村民对高品质舒适生活的诉求，改建村中废弃公共空间，置入餐厅、清吧，在乡村空间中融入部分城市功能；保留乡村崇祀传统，修复土地庙，实现乡村风俗活动的传承和延续。以城乡居民的实际生活为抓手，去粗取精，提升原住村民生活水平的同时满足城市居民消费需求。

此外，进一步进行村庄"水"资源挖掘，在保护生态空间的前提下开发水域新功能。其中，通过拓展"古渡口"文化内涵，重新沟通水系，形成水上游线，在现代化社会中重温圩区传统"水上交通"；在河道、沟渠等水生态环境较高的地区，退渔还水，以水生观光植物打造特色河道缓坡景观，涵养水源；以保护为出发点，修复并改善乡村生态环境，提升生态功能及服务价值，延续人和自然有机融合的乡村空间关系。

Based on the rural society, the design integrates modern civilization, creating a village space with regional characteristics and nostalgia by responding to the renovation strategies of water ecological space, rural production space, and residential living space.

Firstly, by improving the village's agricultural production function, the traditional production space and the landscape space are combined.

Secondly, to meet the living needs of the villagers and urban residents, incorporate urban-level service functions into the rural landscape. Including the addition of villagers' bookstores to meet the needs of villagers' gatherings and cultural needs. Waterfront homestays and service centers have been added by extracting the traditional lifestyle of "living on the water". To respond to villagers' demands for high-quality and comfortable life, the abandoned buildings are renovated by inserting restaurants and bars, integrating urban functions into rural spaces. The reparation of temple of Land God realizes the inheritance and continuation of village customs and activities.

In addition, further excavation of "water" resources in villages will be carried out to develop new functions of water areas on the premise of protecting ecological space. Firstly, by expanding the cultural connotation of the "Ancient Ferry", water transportation in the polder area in a modern society is reappeared. In areas where ecological benefits are significant, aquatic sightseeing plants have been applied to create a characteristic river slope landscape and conserve water.

▲ 钱家渡鸟瞰　The Birdview of the Village

渡

以水为脉，串联新景　River-Linked Scenery

"古渡"风貌承载着钱家渡的自然生态特征和历史文化底蕴。设计首先以村域范围内的河道、渡塘、码头为切入点，恢复水域生态系统，再塑滨水空间。

水域生态修复。通过重点水域的清淤，对现状自然驳岸进行清理和保护，保留原生树木，结合水体条件种植功能不同的水生植物，打造滨水景观。

重置水上交通。设计通过重点河道、沟渠的退渔还水，沟通村庄南部水系和东部水系，利用村域范围内北干沟开辟水上游线，重拾原住村民的集体记忆的同时营造令游客印象深刻的圩区渡口特色。

创新古渡特色活动。依托古渡历史和水文化资源，带动乡村社区感的提升。其中，水岸码头成为承载渡口文化记忆的传统乡村公共空间。设计中临水布置民宿、餐饮、休闲清吧功能，其建筑设计尽可能利用水景特色，让人们在参与特定活动时可随处体验水乡氛围。

"Ancient ferry" carries the natural ecological characteristics and historical and cultural details of Qianjiadu. The design starts with restoring the water ecosystem and reshaping the waterfront space.

Ecological restoration of waters. Through the dredging of key water areas, the current revetment is cleaned and protected, aquatic plants with different functions are planted referring to water body conditions to create a waterfront landscape.

Reset water traffic. The design communicates the southern and eastern water systems of the village, uses the Beigan Ditch to open up the water Route, regaining the collective memory of the villagers as well as creating a polder that impresses tourists.

Innovate the special activities. Relying on history and water culture resources, it promotes the sense of rural community. Among them, the waterfront wharf has become a traditional rural public space that carries the cultural memory of the ferry. All tourist spots are arranged by the water, with architectural design making use of water features as much as possible. The atmosphere of the water town is featured everywhere when participating in specific activities.

02 规划 Planning

▲ 水岸码头 Waterfront Wharf

▼ 水上游线 Water Route

以农为基,三产联动　Agriculture-Based Industries

作为村庄整体风貌的基底,第三产业置入后,农田有潜力承担更多的复合功能。设计在保护基本农田红线的前提下,融合农业生产和田园景观,三产并举,提升农田附加价值的同时实现乡村田园风貌提升。

基本农田保育性提升。设计中对水稻大田进行简单清理,由职业农民耕种,主要田埂道路上种植蔬菜、花卉,堤顶路和旅游道路提供良好的观赏视角。

社区菜园体验式景观设计。设计团队对村内院落进行重新规划,利用蔬菜和果蔬构建村庄景观,采用乡土材料制作篱笆、支架。社区菜园可以提供体验性活动,深度融合农事、童玩、食趣,重拾乡村生活乐趣。

生态富育型观光花田置入。对于村庄周边缺乏种植条件的土地,设计中尝试置入景观花田,采用较为粗放的种植方式,使其在融入乡村风貌的同时增加景观丰富度;兼具生产、生态和观光属性的景观花田水生种植,创造乡村新景。

After the tertiary industry is placed, farmland has the potential to assume more complex functions. Under the premise of protecting the red line of basic farmland, the design integrates agricultural production and pastoral landscape, enhances the added value of farmland while improving rural pastoral view.

Basic farmland has been improved while protected. The rice fields are simply cleaned up and cultivated by professional farmers. Vegetables and flowers planted on the main ridge roads create unique landscape, with the top road and the tourist road to be an excellent viewing angle.

Community vegetable gardens have become a landscape offering farming experience. Community vegetable gardens can provide experiential activities that deeply integrate farming, children's play, and food fun to regain the fun of rural life.

Site sightseeing flower fields for ecological demands. For the land which is not suitable for argriculture, the design attempts to place landscape flower fields and adopts rough planting methods aiming to blend into the countryside. The landscape flower fields with rich attributes are combined with aquatic planting to create a new rural scene.

02 规划　Planning

▲ 北侧透视　Perspective from North

▼ 南侧透视　Perspective from South

居

以人为本，汇联新城　Life-Oriented Construction

村庄转型更新后的钱家渡特色田园乡村，其面向的人群已由纯粹的农民转向了由原住村民、乡村经营者、城市游客构成的新的乡村社群。所以，当下的乡村生活空间呈现出高度城乡融合。在村庄聚落整体风貌的营造中，设计团队通过乡土色彩和材料的现代转译，以及专业指导下一般民舍的村民自主更新，平衡当下城乡居民的不同审美和生活需求，构建城乡融合共享的乡村生活空间。

村落整体风貌的改造在总体上遵循江宁地区典型的"水－田－宅－院"的格局特点。在对大量江南水乡的色彩特征进行汇总和提取后，设计团队确定了以"灰－白－黄"为主色调的整体风貌。在保留村庄自然肌理的基础上，对村内建筑现状进行分类评估，视建筑质量和价值进行拆除、修缮、改建或新建。

After the transformation and renewal of the village, the actual users of Qianjiadu have changed from pure farmers to a new rural community composed of aborigines, rural operators and urban tourists. Therefore, the living space presents a high degree of urban-rural integration. In the construction of the overall style of the village settlement, the design team using modern translation of rural colours and materials, as well as the independent renewal of ordinary houses under professional guidance, managed to balance the different aesthetic and life needs of current urban and rural residents, and build a rural life that is integrated and shared between cities and countrysides.

The transformation of the overall style of the village generally follows the typical pattern of "water-field-house-yard" in Jiangning. After summarizing and extracting the colour characteristics of a large number of Jiangnan water villages, the design team determined the overall style with "grey-white-yellow" as the main color. The current situation of the buildings in the village is classified and assessed, leading to demolishment, reparation or reconstruction depending on the quality and value of the buildings.

02 规划 Planning

活态生活 Present Lifestyle ▶

▼ 民舍组团 Residential Houses

03 建筑
Architecture

03 建筑 Architecture

滨水民宿　Waterside Homestay

占地面积：813 m²
建筑面积：636 m²
完成时间：2018 年

滨水民宿坐落于钱家渡主体水面北部，原为两栋分离的民居，经设计成了主客共享的滨水良居，并结合滨水空间，创造钱家渡的一个码头节点，带动滨水活动的趣味性与连贯性，形成钱家渡整体村落环境中的设计亮点和重要空间节点。

在功能策划的考量上，考虑到城乡产业的融合发展，钱家渡凭借便利的交通位置和优越的景观资源，可以续接城市旅游休闲产业。因此，滨水民宿主要承接针对游客的住宿、餐饮和休闲娱乐功能，并与其他重点建筑以公共服务的共建共享为功能核心，组织生活设施与公共活动，串联整体村域环境。

同时，设计通过保留乡村的风貌形态，建构出乡村记忆的在地表达。首先，设计在原有建筑基础上进行改造扩建，通过二层置入前后两处体量联系两栋民居；其次，设计在原有的平屋顶上进行加建，以坡屋顶的传统建筑形式语言呼应周边建筑，并作为特色的双层 Loft "摘星客房"使用。最后，设计在保留原有门窗关系的基础上，使用充满乡村记忆的当地材料，如青砖、木材等，强化建筑造型的体量关系。

The waterside homestay is located in the northern part of the main water surface. Originally, it was a residential house with two separate buildings. By design, it has become a waterfront residence shared by the host and guests. It creates a dock node of Qianjiadu.

In terms of the function planning, considering the integration of urban and rural industries, Qianjiadu can continue the urban tourism and leisure industry by the virtue of convenient transportation location and superior landscape resources. Therefore, it mainly undertakes the functions of accommodation, catering, leisure and entertainment for tourists. What's more, it takes the co-construction and sharing of public services with other key buildings as the core function.

At the same time, the design constructs the rural memory of the local expression by retaining the style and form of the countryside. Firstly, the design connects the two residential buildings through the placement of two volumes. Secondly, the design changes the original flat roof with a sloping roof. Finally, on the basis of retaining the original doors and windows, the design uses local materials such as black brick, wood, etc.

◀ 整体透视　Overall Perspective

▲ 南侧透视　Perspective from South

▲ 河岸透视　Perspective from the Bank

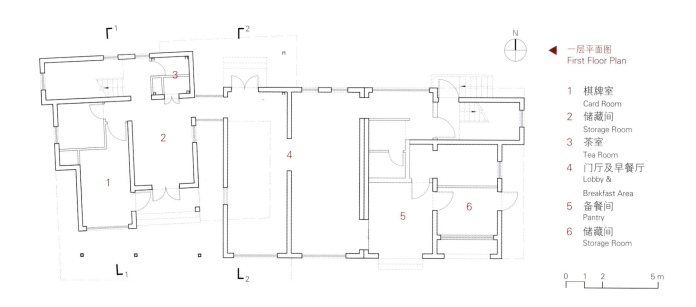

◀ 一层平面图
First Floor Plan

1　棋牌室
　　Card Room
2　储藏间
　　Storage Room
3　茶室
　　Tea Room
4　门厅及早餐厅
　　Lobby &
　　Breakfast Area
5　备餐间
　　Pantry
6　储藏间
　　Storage Room

03 建筑 Architecture

▲ Loft 室内　Inside View of Loft

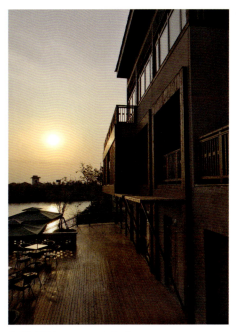

▲ 滨水平台　Waterside Platform

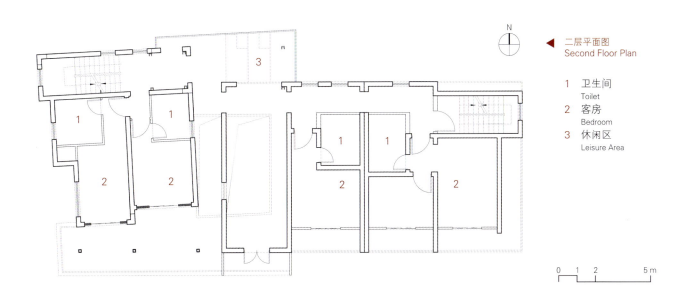

◀ 二层平面图
Second Floor Plan

1　卫生间
　　Toilet
2　客房
　　Bedroom
3　休闲区
　　Leisure Area

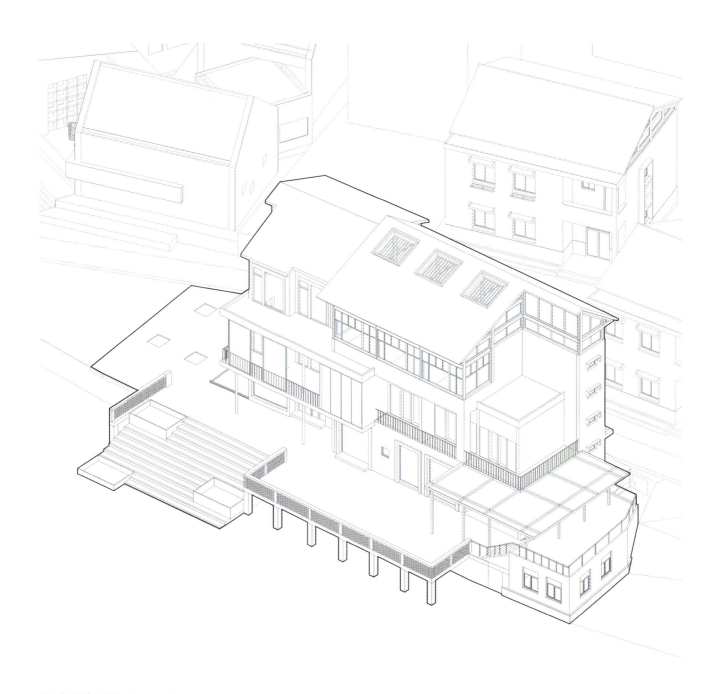

▲ 滨水民宿轴测图　Axonometric

03 建筑 Architecture

▲ 改造过程　Reconstruction Process

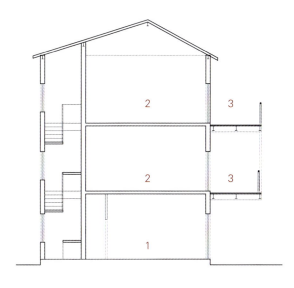

▲ 1-1 剖面　1-1 Section

1　棋牌室 Card Room
2　客房 Bedroom
3　阳台 Balcony

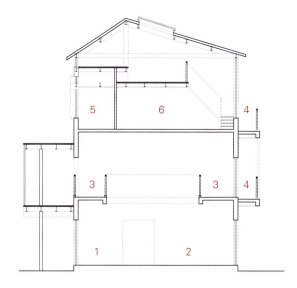

▲ 2-2 剖面　2-2 Section

1　门厅 Lobby
2　早餐厅 Breakfast Area
3　走廊 Corridor
4　阳台 Balcony
5　卫生间 Toilet
6　客房 Bedroom

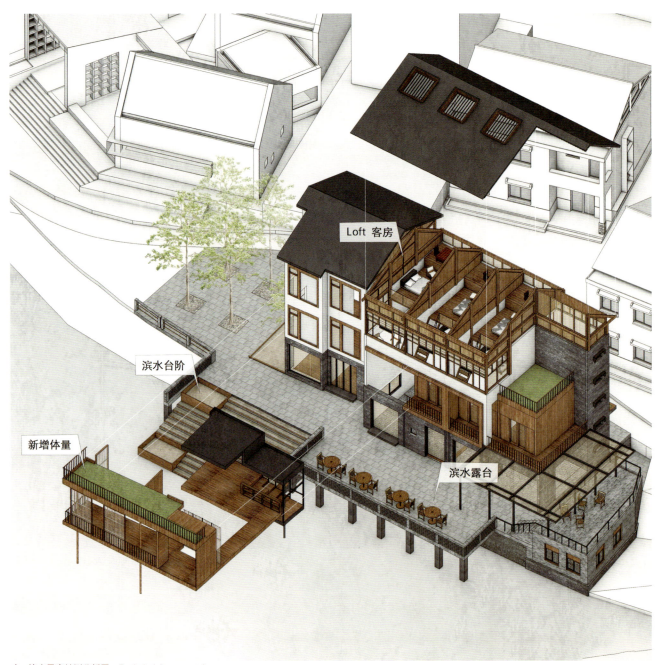

▲ 滨水民宿轴测分析图　Exploded Axonometric

03 建筑　Architecture

Loft 客房

滨水台阶

滨水露台

新增体量

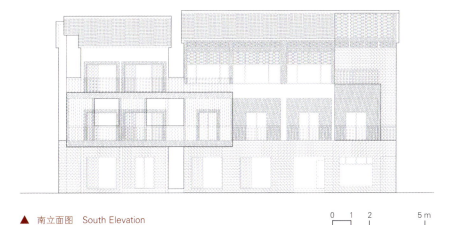

▲ 南立面图　South Elevation

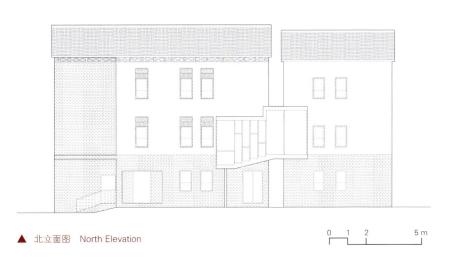

▲ 北立面图　North Elevation

03 建筑　Architecture

民宿服务中心　Homestay Service Center

占地面积：624 m²
建筑面积：350 m²
完成时间：2018 年

民宿服务中心设计采用了新旧并置的原则，以较为开放的姿态积极融入了当地的乡村肌理。作为改造扩建工程，设计在保留原有砖混结构的同时，在内部增设了钢柱作为加固，以保证能够承受新增屋面的荷载。

通过对原有建筑体量的分析和功能的策划，设计将折叠屋面的理念附以原建筑体量，在增加了底层公共空间的同时，提升建筑室内的空间品质。建筑南向沿河面采用了江南传统建筑中花隔扇的形式语言与具有现代感的竖向线条相结合，利用宜人的尺度统一景观与建筑两个部分。北侧采用了简洁的体块穿插手法，面对乡村入口广场形成开放的界面。东侧池塘景观与平台、连廊空间相互映衬，别开生面，成为游客驻足休憩的好去处。

The design of the homestay service center adopts the principle of juxtaposition of the old and the new, and actively integrates the local rural texture with a more open attitude. As a reconstruction and extension project, while retaining the original brick-concrete structure, steel columns were added as reinforcement to ensure that it can bear the load of the new roof.

Through the analysis of the original building volume and the function planning, the design attaches the idea of the folding roof to the original building volume, which increases the public space of the ground floor and improves the space quality of the building interior. The south side along the river of the building adopts the formal language of Jiangnan traditional building and the modern vertical line, and unifies the landscape and the building with a pleasant scale. The north side adopts a concise volume interspersing technique, forming an open interface to the village entrance square. The pond landscape on the east side is set off by the terrace and corridor space, which makes it a good place for tourists to stop and rest.

◀ 南侧主入口透视　Perspective of South Main Entrance

03 建筑　Architecture

▲ 东北侧透视　Perspective from Northeast

▲ 北侧透视　Perspective from North

◀ 东南侧透视　Perspective from Southeast

▲ 二层室内　Inside View of the Second Floor

檐下空间　View under the Eaves ▶

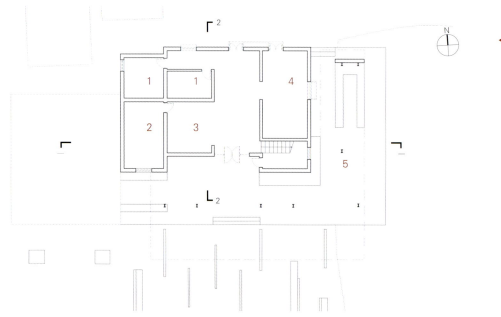

◀ 一层平面图
First Floor Plan

1　卫生间
　　Toilet
2　办公室
　　Office
3　咨询服务室
　　Consultation Service Room
4　茶室
　　Tea Room
5　露台
　　Terrace

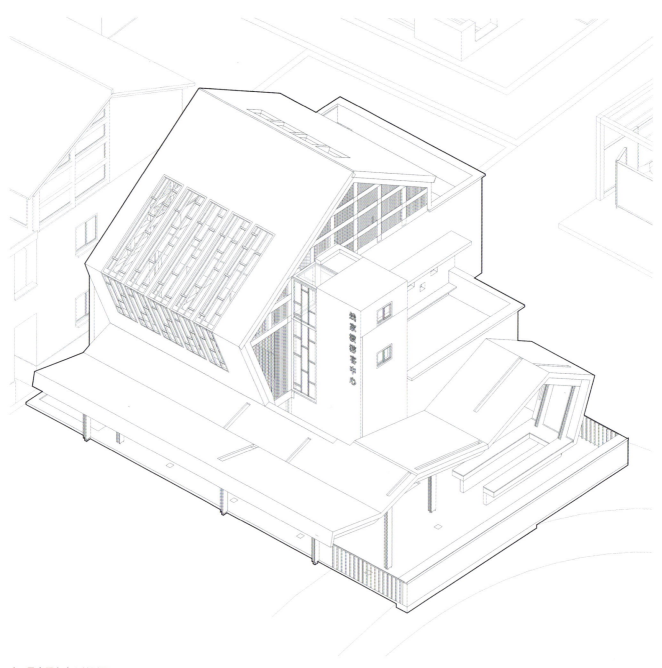

▲ 民宿服务中心轴测图　Axonometric

03 建筑　Architecture

▲　改造过程　Reconstruction Process

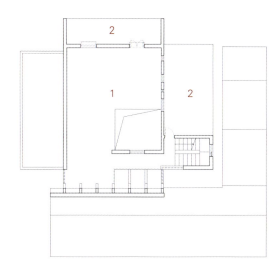

◀　二层平面图
Second Floor Plan

1　茶室
　　Tea Room
2　观景平台
　　Sightseeing Platform

0　1　2　　　5 m

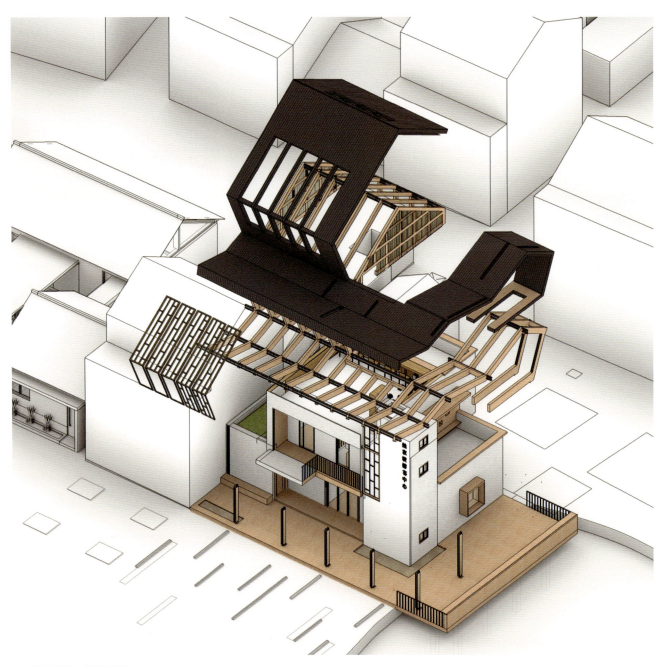

▲ 民宿服务中心轴测分析图 Exploded Axonometric

03 建筑 Architecture

坡顶

立面

边廊

雨棚

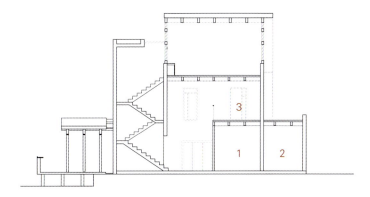

▲ 1–1 剖面 1–1 Section

1 办公室 Office
2 咨询服务室 Consultation Service Room
3 茶室 Tea Room

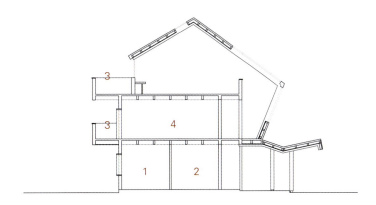

▲ 2–2 剖面 2–2 Section

1 卫生间 Toilet
2 咨询服务室 Consultation Service Room
3 观景平台 Sightseeing Platform
4 茶室 Tea Room

63

03 建筑 Architecture

乡村书屋　Village Reading Room

占地面积：578 m²
建筑面积：304 m²

完成时间：2018 年

乡村书屋位于村内临近水域的位置。原场地破旧房屋被拆除，因此本项目利用原有拆除建筑的老砖材料，结合新的空间体系，在原址上进行新建筑的设计建造。

书屋结合原有乡村建筑体量尺度与肌理特性，通过自身体量与结构秩序的重组，创造室内、室外以及乡村邻里的共享空间。其中，公共的停留休憩空间和室内面向水面的空间，则以建筑的方式"框"景乡村，实现从"在乡村阅读"到"阅读乡村"。即如建筑临水立面的连续条窗设计，与水景及对岸建筑产生视觉上的关联与呼应。此外，书屋将建筑的支撑结构与室内家具相结合，以书架为限定要素对建筑体量与室内空间进行划分与空间转折的限定，以此创造不同功能空间的序列性。

整体而言，书屋在原有体量基础上，提供了乡村阅读的场所，留出了乡村公共空间，在构建钱家渡村民公共场所的同时，为乡村空间置入了新的活力。

The village reading room is located in the water area of the village. The old buildings on the original site were demolished, so the new building was designed and built on the original site by using the old brick materials of the old demolished buildings.

The reading room combines the scale and texture of the original rural building to create the shared space of indoor, outdoor and rural neighborhood through the reorganization of its own volume and structural order. Among them, the public space facing the water is built to "frame" the countryside from "reading in the countryside" to "reading the countryside". Take the continuous strip window design for instance, it has visual relation with the waterscape and the opposite bank building. In addition, it combines the supporting structure of the building with the interior furniture, divides the building volume and the interior space with the bookcase.

On the whole, the reading room provides a place for reading in the countryside and a public space in the countryside. While constructing the public place for villagers, it puts new vitality into the rural space.

◀ 河岸透视　Perspective from the Bank

▲ 东侧透视
Perspective from East

◄ 西侧透视　Perspective from West
▼ 入口透视　Perspective of the Entrance

▲ 室内空间　Inside View

▲ 室外廊道　Outdoor Corridor

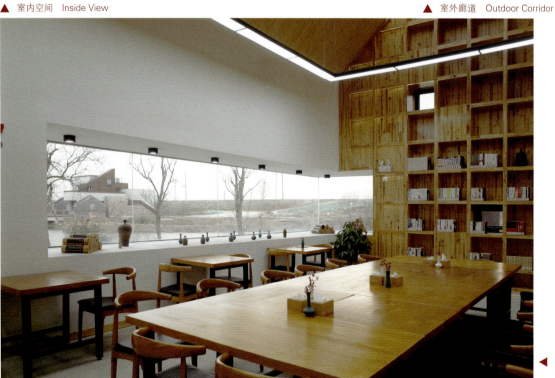
◀ 转角景窗
Corner Window

▼▲ 水平条窗内外景　The Inner and Outdoor View of the Strip Window

03 建筑　Architecture

▲ 入口景框内外景　The Inner and Outdoor View of the Entrance

▲ 立面细节 Details of Elevations

▲ 室内空间 Inside View

03 建筑　Architecture

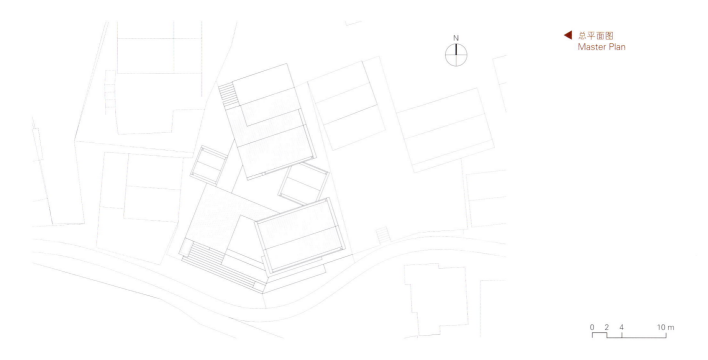

◀ 总平面图
Master Plan

▲ 西南侧鸟瞰　Birdview from Southeast

▲ 入口通道透视　Perspective of the Entrance Passage

73

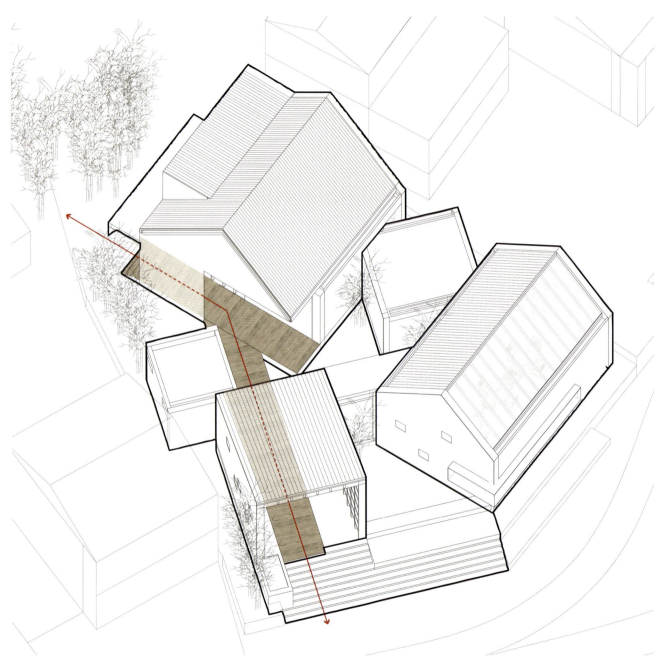

▲ 村民书屋轴测图　Axonometric

03 建筑　Architecture

▲　建造过程　Construction Process

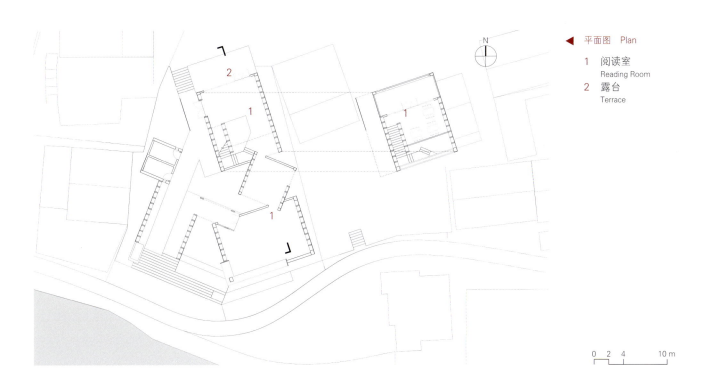

◀　平面图　Plan

1　阅读室　Reading Room
2　露台　Terrace

0　2　4　10 m

▲ 村民书屋轴测分析图　Exploded Axonometric

03 建筑 Architecture

木制饰面

竹饰立面

内部砖饰

青砖体量

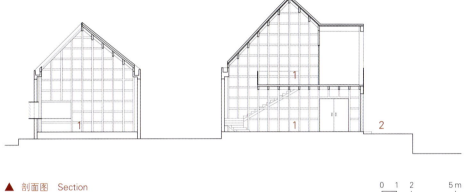

▲ 剖面图　Section
1　阅读室 Reading Room
2　露台 Terrace

0　1　2　　　5 m

▲ 西立面图　West Elevation

0　1　2　　　5 m

77

03　建筑　Architecture

水上餐厅　Waterfront Restaurant

占地面积：1290 m²
建筑面积：1279 m²

完成时间：2019 年

水上餐厅原址为长条形状的乡村小学校，该项目在设计中顺应原乡村滨水建筑的形态，形成具有公共性的长条水上餐厅。

面向开阔的湖面，水上餐厅形成了对其视线、景观和活动在垂直方向上的不同呼应。在视线设计上，首层强化视线向室外水面的延伸，二层则是将人流引向高层，为游客提供了面向水面和整体村庄的俯视景观视角。在景观设计上，首层将滨水平台延伸至水面，拉近与景观的距离，二层则是形成屋顶绿化种植，将建筑融入景观之中。在活动方面，首层开放平面为更加公共的就餐空间，二层则为插入体块内部的包间，具备一定的私密性。

在设计中，建筑底层立面为大面积的玻璃幕墙，模糊了建筑内部空间与外部滨水平台的界限，并将室外的水景纳入室内，视线上实现了空间水平向的不断延伸。建筑二层则是在以统一的体块插入的形体操作模式下，形成了公共空间和就餐包间的划分，并与外部表现统一，形成了屋顶的起伏，提供了屋顶休憩平台的同时，丰富了村庄整体的第五立面。

The waterfront restaurant was originally a rural primary school. The project was designed in accordance with the form of the original building, forming a long strip waterfront restaurant.

Facing the lake, the waterfront restaurant forms different echoes in the vertical orientation of its views, landscapes and activities. In the sight line design, the first floor strengthens the extension of the sight line to the outdoor water surface; the second floor is to flow the people to the upper level, providing tourists with the bird's eye views. In the landscape design, the first floor extends the waterfront platform to the water, closing the distance with the landscape; the second floor is to form a roof planting. In terms of activities, the first floor is open for public dining space, while the second floor has internal private compartments .

In the design, the ground floor facade is a large glass curtain wall, which weakens the boundary between the internal space and the external waterfront platform, and integrates the outdoor water scene into the interior. On the second floor, it forms the division of the public space and the dining room .

◀ 西北侧透视　Perspective from Northwest

▲ 北侧透视　Perspective from North

03 建筑 Architecture

▲ 二层平台透视　Perspective of 2nd Floor Platform

▲ 二层平台透视　Perspective of 2nd Floor Platform

▲ 西南侧透视　Perspective from Southwest

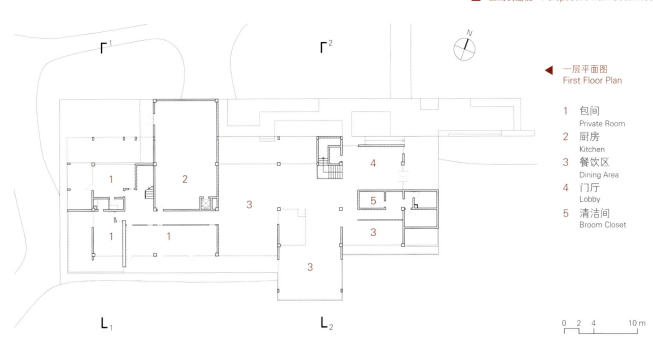

◀ 一层平面图
First Floor Plan

1　包间
　　Private Room
2　厨房
　　Kitchen
3　餐饮区
　　Dining Area
4　门厅
　　Lobby
5　清洁间
　　Broom Closet

▲ 北侧透视　Perspective from North

03 建筑 Architecture

▲ 二层室内　Inside View of the Second Floor

▲ 庭院空间　View of the Courtyard

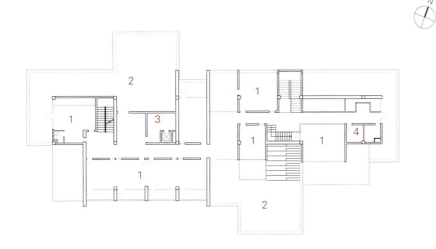

◀ 二层平面图
Second Floor Plan

1　包间
　　Private Room
2　露台
　　Terrace
3　备餐间
　　Servery
4　卫生间
　　Toilet

◀ 南侧透视　Perspective from South
▼ 落地景窗　French Windows

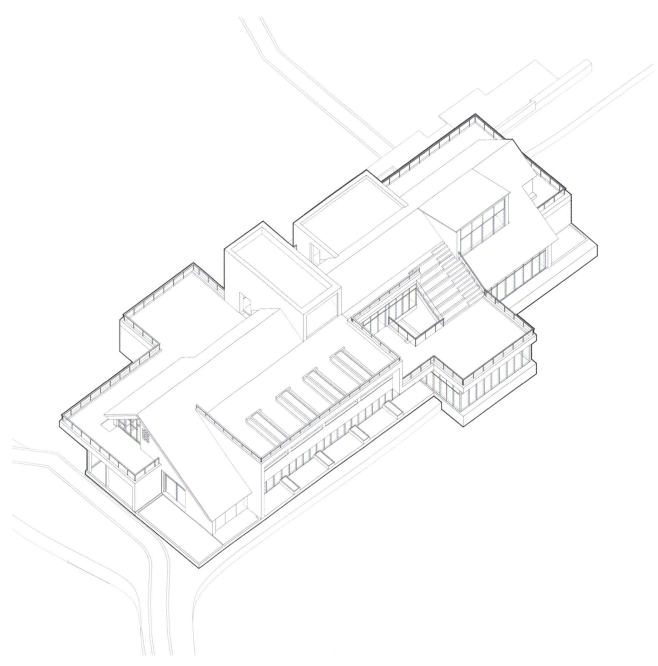

▲ 水上餐厅轴测图　Axonometric

03 建筑 Architecture

▲ 建造过程　Construction Process

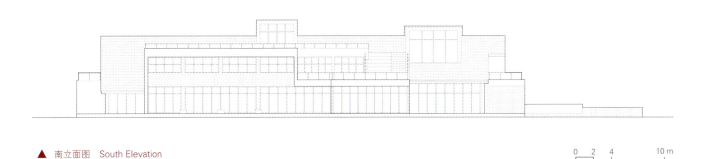

▲ 南立面图　South Elevation

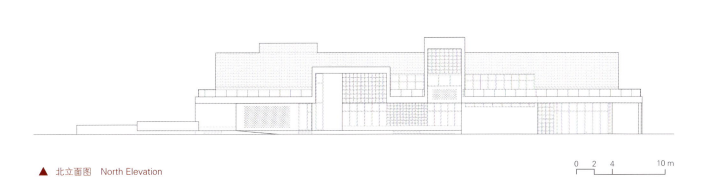

▲ 北立面图　North Elevation

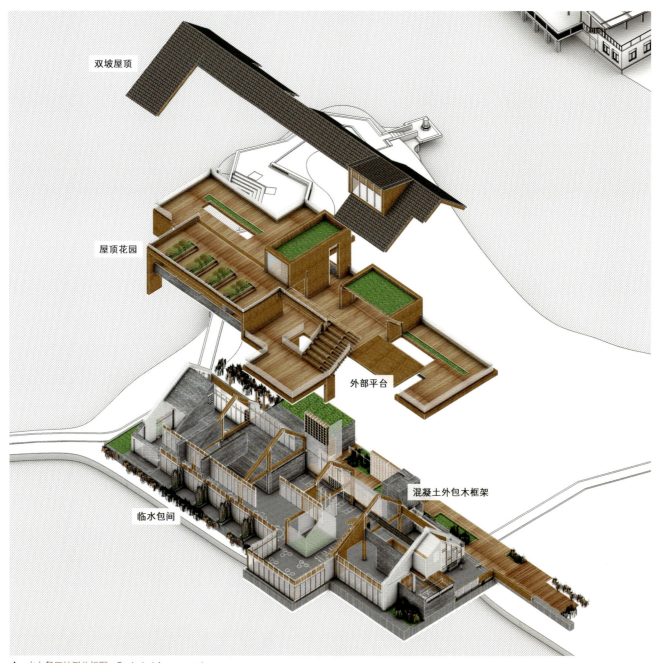

▲ 水上餐厅轴测分析图　Exploded Axonometric

03 建筑 Architecture

双坡屋顶

屋顶花园

外部平台

临水包间

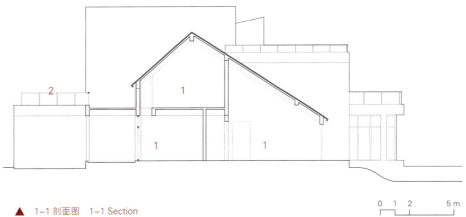

▲ 1-1 剖面图　1-1 Section

    1　包间　Private Room
    2　露台　Terrace

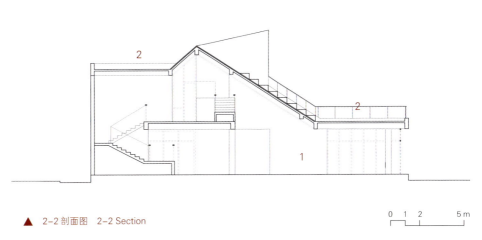

▲ 2-2 剖面图　2-2 Section

    1　餐饮区　Dining Area
    2　露台　Terrace

03 建筑　Architecture

水岸清吧　Waterside Pub

占地面积：620 m²
建筑面积：283 m²
完成时间：2019 年

水岸清吧位于钱家渡村庄的西南角，与村落主题隔水相望。清吧结合原乡村水泵站的残址进行建设，希望在相对远离村庄本体的位置，设立一个可以举办各种娱乐活动的室内外场所。建筑结合水泵站的砖石和部分墙体，设置专门的陈列区展示水利设施和水利文化。

设计利用新的材料——混凝土和木材，与原有的水泵站的石台、砖墙相互结合，利用木质的入口门廊、楼梯平台围绕包裹着整体建筑，引导游人拾级而上，走上二、三层的观景平台眺望远处的村落和水景。建筑室内、室外两条动线结合成一体，形成从室外到室内互动的连贯流线。这使清吧不仅具备基本使用功能，也在成为滨水看与被看的节点同时，成为可供游览体验的景观；而临水挑出的亲水驳岸，与滨水民宿一样，承接着钱家渡水上游览路线的站点功能，让人们可以在几个重要的公共建筑之间，通过水上通路进行关联。

The waterside pub is located in the southwest corner of the village. We hope to set up an indoor and outdoor place which can hold all kinds of recreational activities in the place far away from the village itself. The building has a special display area displaying water facilities and water culture combined with the masonry of the pumping station and part of the walls.

The design uses new materials—concrete and wood, combined with the stone table and brick walls of the original pumping station and wraps the building around a wooden entrance porch and stair deck to guide visitors up the stairs. Visitors can walk up to the second or third floor platform to overlook the villages and water. The two dynamic lines indoors and outdoors integrate, which makes the waterside pub not only have basic use function, but also become the landscape for sightseeing experience. And like the waterfront lodgings, the jetting-out hydrophilic shore continues the Qianjiadu' aquatic tour route, allowing people to connect between several important public buildings via water passages.

◀ 河岸透视　Perspective from the Bank

临水平台　Waterside Platform ▶

▼ 西侧透视　Perspective from West

▶ 北侧透视　Perspective from North

03 建筑 Architecture

▲ 书屋入口远景　View from Reading Room Entrance　　▲ 新旧并置　Juxtaposition of the Old and the New　　▼ 水景透视　Perspective from Water

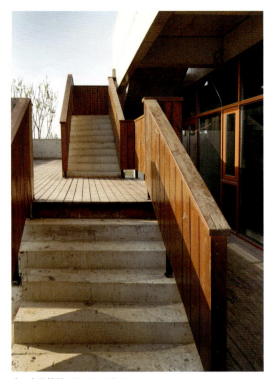

▲ 室外楼梯　Outdoor Staircase

▲ 入口空间　View of the Entrance

▲ 平台透视　Perspective from the Platform

▲ 临水面透视　Perspective from Waterside

◀ 一层平面图
First Floor Plan

1　水利设施展示
　　Exhibition Area
2　餐饮区
　　Dining Area
3　厨房
　　Kitchen
4　包间
　　Private Room
5　室外平台
　　Outdoor Platform

0　1　2　　5 m

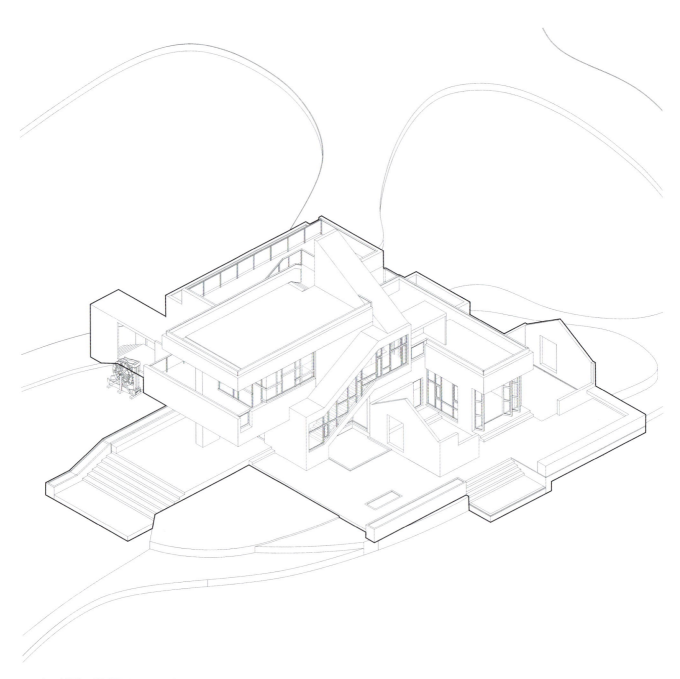

▲ 水岸清吧轴测图　Axonometric

03 建筑 Architecture

▲ 建造过程 Construction Process

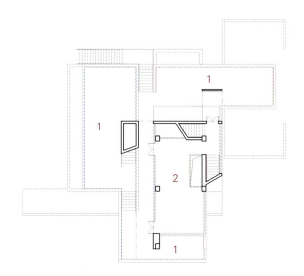

◀ 二层平面图
Second Floor Plan

1 室外平台
　Outdoor Platform
2 餐饮区
　Dining Area

0　1　2　　5 m

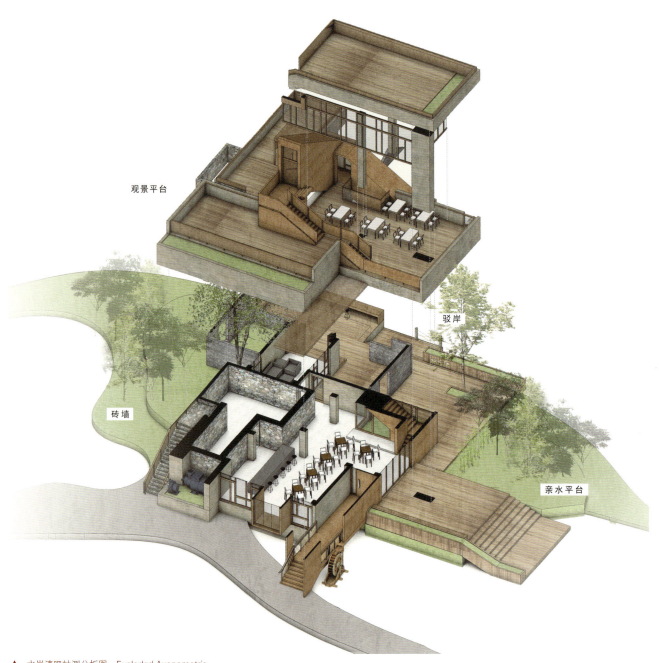

▲ 水岸清吧轴测分析图　Exploded Axonometric

03 建筑　Architecture

观景平台

驳岸

砖墙

亲水平台

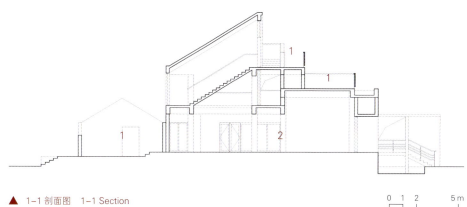

▲ 1-1 剖面图　1-1 Section

  1 室外平台 Outdoor Platform
  2 餐饮区 Dining Area

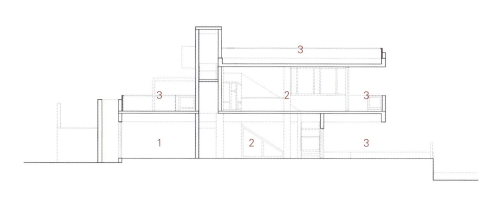

▲ 2-2 剖面图　2-2 Section

  1 卫生间 Toilet
  2 餐饮区 Dining Area
  3 室外平台 Outdoor Platform

03 建筑　Architecture

土地庙　Temple of Land God

占地面积：141 m²
建筑面积：32 m²

完成时间：2018 年

土地庙作为乡村崇祀空间的代表，凝结了村民们的集体记忆，是乡村传统公共生活的重要载体。钱家渡土地庙的重建，在尊重原有村民的习俗和意愿的同时，结合现代化的建构方式和设计语言，营造了具有当代新乡村特质的场所与空间。

在前期调研村民访谈有关土地庙的话题时，谈论最多的便是内部祭祀的空间、位置和公共活动。可见，村民对于土地庙的认识和记忆同样可以从空间、场所以及功能三个方面构建。空间、场所以及功能的差异导致两个土地庙形成特殊的集体记忆和场所精神。在设计中，建造技术的更迭和材料的更换并未影响村民对于庙宇的集体认同，而屋顶稍微变化的引入光线，为土地庙空间带来不同的空间感知。

建造过程中，当地木工师傅结合自己的经验，对木结构进行了一定的自我调节，增强了木结构的在地性，这使得土地庙建设在现代设计与传承技艺之间建立了乡村营建的平衡点。

As a representative of worship space in the countryside, the temple coagulates the collective memory, being an important carrier of the traditional public life.

When the villagers were interviewed about the temple of land god, the most talked topic is the internal worship space, location and public activities. The differences of space, place and function lead to the formation of collective memory and place spirit. In the design, the alternation of construction techniques and the replacement of materials didn't affect the villagers' collective identification, while the roof slightly changed to introduce light, bringing a different spatial perception.

During the construction process, the local carpenters made some self-adjustment to the timber structure, which enhanced the local character of the timber structure. This made the construction of the temple of Land God set up the balance point of rural construction between modern designs and inheritance techniques.

◀ 西侧透视　Perspective from West

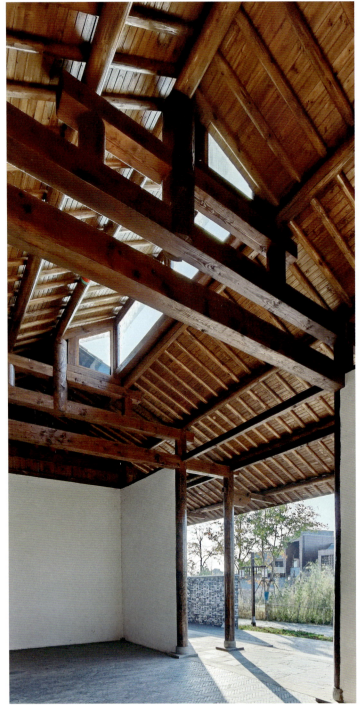

▲ 室内空间　Inside View

▲ 边廊空间　Corridor View

03 建筑 Architecture

▼ 南侧透视　Perspective from South

西南侧透视　Perspective from Southwest ▶

◀　屋架细节　Details of the Roof
▼　南侧透视　Perspective from South

03 建筑 Architecture

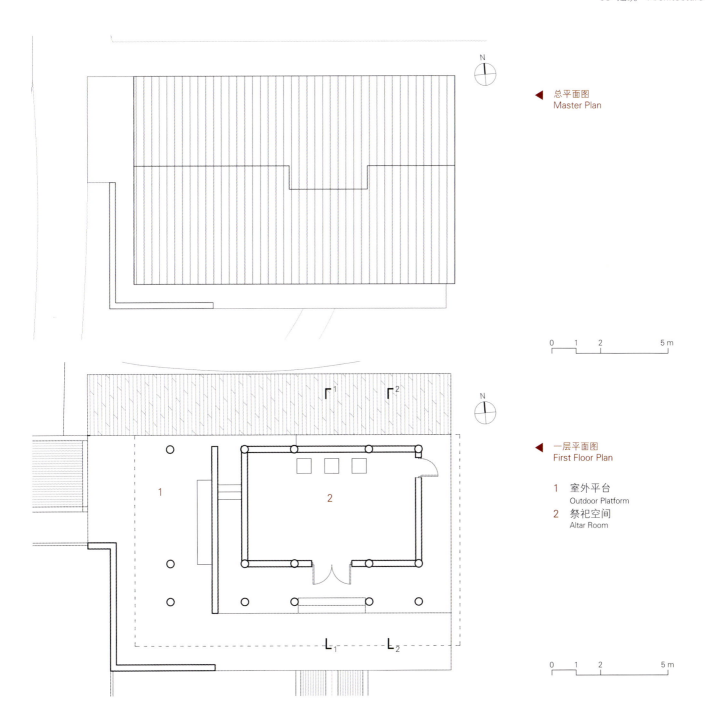

总平面图
Master Plan

一层平面图
First Floor Plan

1 室外平台
　Outdoor Platform
2 祭祀空间
　Altar Room

111

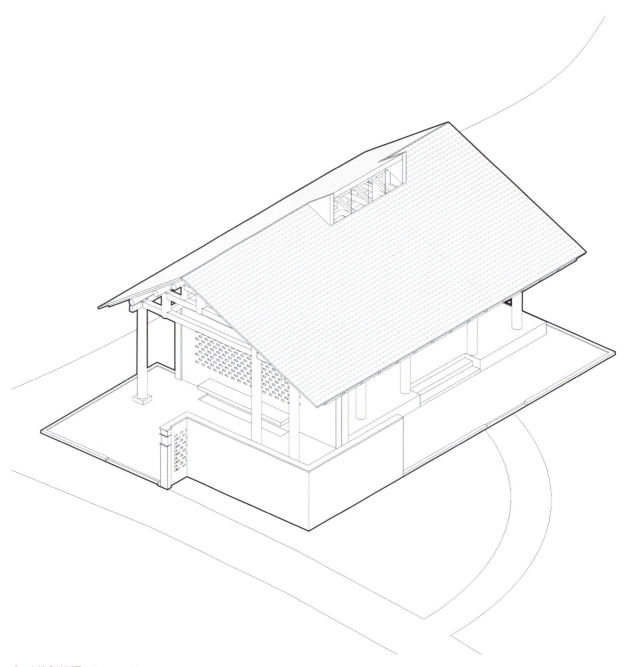

▲ 土地庙轴测图　Axonometric

03 建筑 Architecture

▲ 建造过程　Construction Process

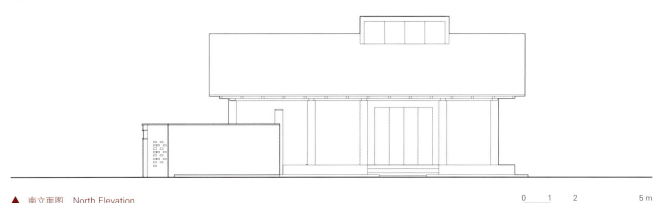

▲ 南立面图　North Elevation

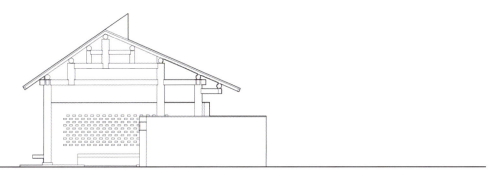

▲ 西立面图　West Elevation

▲ 土地庙爆炸轴测图　Exploded Axonometric

03 建筑　Architecture

天窗

抬梁屋架

拼砖墙面

折板片墙

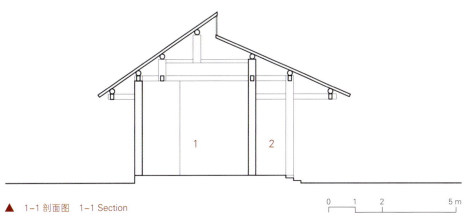

▲ 1-1 剖面图　1-1 Section

　　1　祭祀空间 Altar Room
　　2　檐下空间 Space under the Eaves

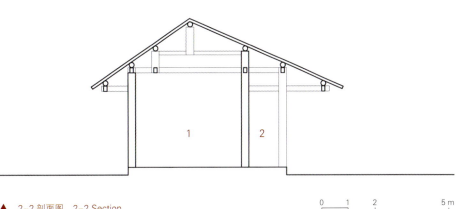

▲ 2-2 剖面图　2-2 Section

　　1　祭祀空间 Altar Room
　　2　檐下空间 Space under the Eaves

03 建筑 Architecture

乡村生活馆　Village Life Hall

占地面积：251 m²
建筑面积：123 m²

完成时间：2018 年

乡村生活馆位于钱家渡村中部，东侧紧邻钱家渡游客中心，西侧与水边民宿隔街相望。展览馆原为两栋独立的青砖房，建设时间不可考。设计团队经调研后认为其具有一定历史价值且传统建造工艺保留较完好，但长时间空置导致房屋结构与屋顶已存在一定程度破损。

设计团队依据现状决定从三方面提出改造策略。其一，对原房屋结构进行加固，更换和修补破损的屋顶和墙面，尽量保持建造工艺与材料的在地性；其二，通过替换原有门窗、山墙开洞等方式改善房屋的采光、通风等性能，注重新增构件的材料与原房屋相一致，有效提升房屋舒适度的同时保持其历史感；其三，设计重构了两幢房屋周边的公共空间，木构连廊将两座青砖房相连并形成标志性的入口灰空间，廊下则成为乡村生活的展示场所与村民休闲的活动空间。改造后的青砖房转化为集展览活动和休闲活动于一体的乡村生活展览馆，成为村内一处多元开放、主客共享的代表性公共节点。

The Village Life Hall is located in the middle of the village. The Hall was two independent black brick houses originally. After investigation, the design team concluded that it had historical value. However, parts of the house had been damaged due to long-term vacancy.

Based on the status quo, the design team raised some transformation strategies. First, reinforce the original structure of the house, replace and repair the damaged roof and walls. Second, by replacing the original doors and windows, opening the Gable Wall and so on, we can improve the performance of lighting and ventilation of the house. Third, the design reconstructs the public space around the two houses. The wooden corridor connects the two black brick houses and forms a symbolic grey space at the entrance while the space under the corridor becomes the village life exhibition place and the villager leisure activity space. After the transformation, the Village Life Hall has become a representative public node of a multi-open, host-and-guestshare.

◀ 整体透视　Overall Perspective

03 建筑　Architecture

◀ 木构连廊外景　The Outdoor View of the Wooden Corridor
▼ 木构连廊内景　The Inner View of the Wooden Corridor

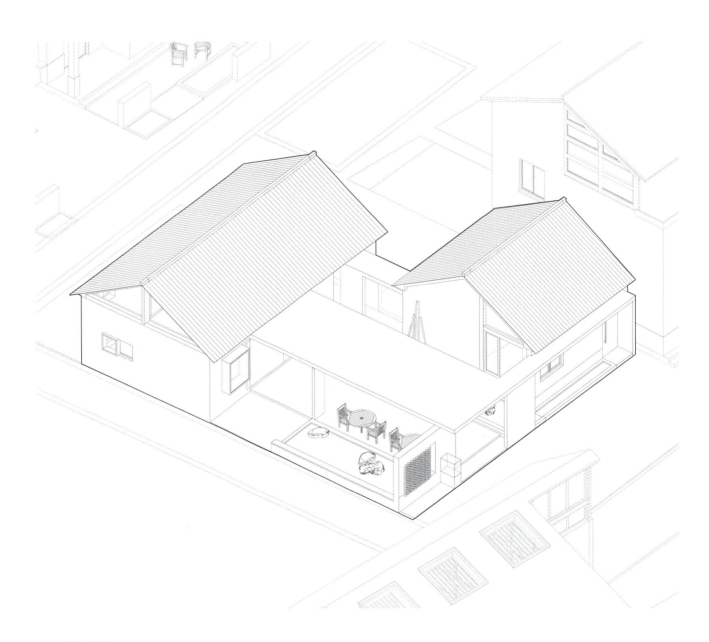

▲ 乡村生活馆轴测图　Axonometric

03 建筑　Architecture

▲　改造过程　Reconstruction Process

▼　木构展廊　Wooden Exhibition Corridor

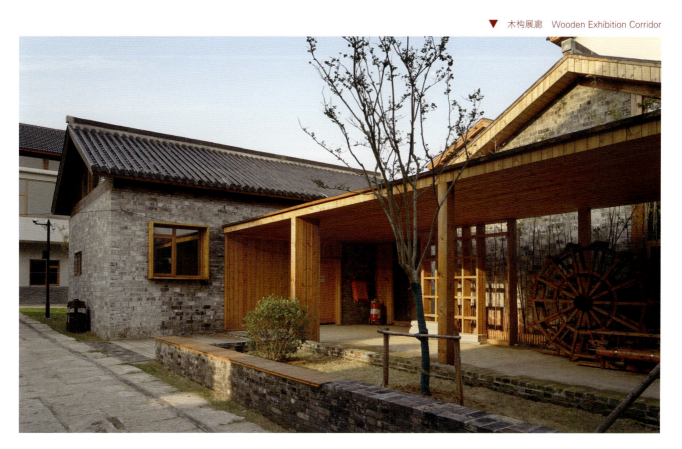

123

▲ 乡村生活馆轴测分析图　Exploded Axonometric

03 建筑 Architecture

落地景窗

屋架新用

木饰窗框

木制展廊

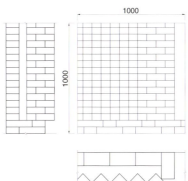
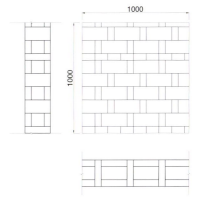

▲ 砖砌大样　Brick Details

04 导则
Renovation Guideline

04 导则 Renovation Guideline

专业指导与自主建设结合的民舍改造建议
Suggestions Based on the Combination of Professional Guidance and Independent Construction

对一般民舍进行更新时，设计团队采用了"范例样式＋村民自主发挥"的综合更新方式。钱家渡的新建民舍虽然在材料和细节上区别较大，但体量和基本模式非常相似。设计从中抽象出民舍的基本样式，在色彩、材料、基本做法的整体把控下，对界面、山墙、门窗、围墙、院落等建筑要素提出多种改造样式，保障民舍功能转换的灵活性和潜力。具体操作上，按照民舍所处位置、现状情况和未来规划定位对其改造方式进行建议。对于所处位置沿街、人流量大的民舍建议通过多种手法增加底层沿街公共空间，活跃氛围，为整体风貌增加层次；对于其他民舍，建议相邻民舍考虑不同的改造模式，增加差异性；有院落保存较好的民舍，建议保存院落，结合未来功能进行设计。

为了避免统一改造对实际使用者需求的忽视，在实际建造中专业设计者鼓励当地村民和未来的钱家渡经营者进行民舍的自主建设。这样，业主可以根据自身需求选择建筑要素的不同改造样式。而实际使用者也可以在不破坏村庄整体风貌的前提下在产权范围内发挥能动性进行自我创造，保留差异性，增强参与感，实现村庄整体风貌的和而不同。

The design team adopted a comprehensive renewal method of "model style + villagers' independent play" in individual farmhouse renewal. The design abstracts the basic style of residential houses, which are quite similar compared to the difference of material. Under the overall control of colours, materials and basic practices, a variety of transformation styles are proposed for architectural elements such as interfaces, gables, doors and windows, etc., ensuring the flexibility of functional conversion of residential houses. In terms of specific operations, transformation methods of each farmhouse are suggested according to their location, quality and future planning. Three kinds of farmhouses have been classified Advises are proposed referring to different conditions.

In order to avoid ignoring the needs of actual users in the unified renovation, professional designers encourage local villagers and future operators to carry out independent construction of houses. In this way, the owner can choose different renovation styles according to their own needs. The actual users can also play their initiative within the scope of property rights to create themselves without destroying the overall style of the village, retaining differences, enhancing the sense of participation, and achieving harmony and difference in the overall style of the village.

04 导则 Renovation Guideline

04 导则 Renovation Guideline

04 导则 Renovation Guideline

石 Stone		 石砌驳岸	 毛石景墙
木 Wood		 木质门窗 & 饰面	 木构架
砖 Brick		 拼花砖墙	 砖砌栏杆
竹 Bamboo		 竹编篱笆	 竹贴饰面

材料色彩控制导则 ▲
Material Color Control Guidelines

▲ 沿路民舍改造案例　Reconstruction of Residential Buildings along the Road
▼ 不同年代建筑在村内汇集　Buildings of Different Ages Gather in the Village

▲ 非沿街保存较好民舍改造范例
Reconstruction of Well-preserved Residential Buildings

04 导则 Renovation Guideline

04 导则 Renovation Guideline

沿街民宅改造　Reconstruction of Residential Building along the Road ▲
乡村步道　Village Walkway ▶

05 景观
Landscape

▲ 钱家渡村周边环境　Village Surroundings

05 景观　Landscape

水乡钱家渡　Waterside Village Qianjiadu

钱家渡村江南水乡风貌保存较好，景观设计中保留、整理以及改造现有鱼塘、河道等水系，重新建立起自然村落与周边农田、水域的空间关系，呈现出湖熟当地有代表性的体验尺度宜人的特色生态田园空间。

Qianjiadu Village is a well-preserved Jiangnan Water Village. The existing fish ponds, river channels and other water systems are well-preserved, reorganized, and reconstructed in the landscape design. The spatial relationship between the village and surrounding farmland and waters has been re-established, showing the local ecological pastoral space with a pleasant scale.

水系景观　Water System Landscape ▶

▼ 孙家桥村花田　Flower Field of the Village　　　　▲ 孙家桥村远景　Distant View of the Village

05 景观 Landscape

村口景观 Landscape at the Village Entrance

在入村的三个主要人流方向上设置了三处村口景观节点，并配合宣传标语作为入村标志，引导视线与人流。

三组入口景观的共同点为：空间开敞，与周边农田、水系等环境有机融合及延伸成一体。同时，每一处的主景都体量较大，形成室外景观"雕塑"的效果，达到吸引视线的作用。

根据布局方向，村口景观分为：孙家桥村北入口、东入口以及钱家渡村入口。

Three village entrance landscape nodes are set up in the three main directions where people enter the village, with propaganda slogans using as signs of entering the village to guide the sight and the flow of people.

The common feature of the three groups of entrance landscapes is: open space, organic integration and extension with surrounding farmland, water systems and other environments. At the same time, the main scenery of each place is relatively large in volume, forming the effect of the outdoor landscape "sculpture", achieving the effect of attracting sight.

According to the layout direction, the village entrance landscape is divided into: the north entrance, east entrance of Sunjiaqiao Village and the entrance of Qianjiadu Village.

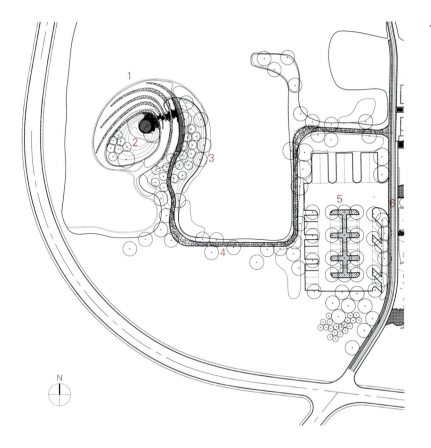

▶ 总平面 Master Plan

1　水石带
　　Water&Stone Belt
2　观景木平台
　　Viewing Wooden Platform
3　桃林
　　Peach Orchard
4　碎石小道
　　Rubble Lane
5　停车场
　　Parking Lot
6　进村道路
　　Road of the Village Entrance

孙家桥村北入口　The North Entrance of Sunjiaqiao Village

对原有岛屿进行整合而得北入口景观，形成大小相异的两块水岛，并以汀步相连接。

大水岛上利用石块与卵石铺装，形成水石环带，成为从北而来游客居高临下观望到的主景。

小水岛上建造平台，结合条石，放置入口标志名牌。视野开阔，也可登岛坐憩。

岛上以桃林为主要背景树种，乡村气息浓厚。下层种植水生植物与观赏水草结合，使入口景观具有野趣，并有生态意义。

The north entrance landscape is the integration of the original islands, and the built landscape forms two water islands of different sizes, which are connected by stepping steps.

The Big Island is paved with stones and pebbles to form a water stonering, which has become the main scenery for tourists from the north. A platform is built on the small island, combined with a stone, and an entrance sign is placed.

With a orchard of peaches as the main background tree species, the Small Island has a strong rural atmosphere. The combination of various ornamental aquatic plants in the lower layer makes the entrance landscape interesting and ecologically meaningful.

05 景观 Landscape

▲ 入口碎石小道 Entrance Gravel Path   ▼ 北入口水石带 Water&Stone Belt of the North Entrance

孙家桥村东入口 The East Entrance of Sunjiaqiao Village

东入口利用场地原有地形高差，整理成微地形，并延伸出坡地景观。以三角形为构图元素，砌筑石挡墙，形成入口具有视觉指向的景观序列。挡墙以村内拆旧的碎石为主，用具有艺术感的砌筑方式加持，朴素而又现代。

同时，场地因地制宜保留了村口原有的大女贞，结合碎石块等铺设道路，成为村口可以驻足停留乘凉的地方。坡底处结合碎石步道和挡墙营造雨水花园，既解决了场地的排水问题，又可以形成一处环境自然的湿地场所景观。

The east entrance uses the original topographical height difference to extend the slope landscape. Using triangles as the composition element and building stone retaining walls, the entrance has a visually directed landscape sequence. The retaining wall is mainly composed of old gravel demolished in the village, blessed with artistic masonry, which is simple and modern.

At the same time, the site retains the original large privet at the entrance of the village according to local conditions, combined with the road paved with gravel. A rainwater garden at the bottom of the slope created not only solves the drainage problem of the site, but also forms a natural wetland landscape.

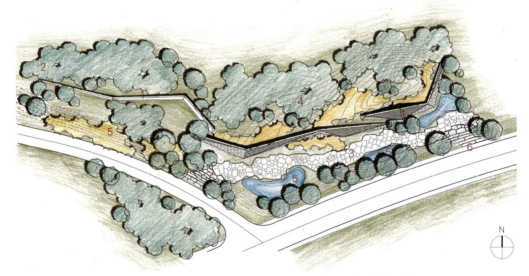

◀ 总平面图
　 Master Plan

1　碎石挡墙　Rubble Retaining Wall
2　现状女贞林　Present Privet Trees
3　碎石铺地　Rubble Paving
4　桃林　Peach Orchard
5　雨水花园带　Rain Garden Belt
6　入口台阶　Entrance Steps

东入口碎石挡墙及铺地　Rubble Retaining Wall and Paving at the East Entrance ▼

▲ 碎石挡墙与大女贞　Rubble Retaining Wall and Privet trees

钱家渡村入口　The Entrance of Qianjiadu Village

钱家渡村入口位于村口道路交叉口西南的视觉焦点上，以竹编构筑物为主景，构筑物象征渔网、竹篓或草垛等多重含义。构筑物下有环形场地，可供观光人群在村头集合停驻。

构筑物通过组群的布置方式成环状，具有一定视觉体量，在尺度上可以与周边开阔田野相称，同时圆形组群又不失为一件稻田中表现"丰收"的大地艺术品。

The entrance of Qianjiadu Village is located in the visual focus of the intersection of the village road. Take bamboo structures as the main scene, the structure symbolizes multiple meanings such as fishing nets, bamboo baskets or haystacks.

Several parts are arranged in groups in a ring shape with a certain visual volume, which can be commensurate with the surrounding open fields in terms of scale. At the same time, the circular group is a piece of land art that expresses the "bumper harvest" in the rice field.

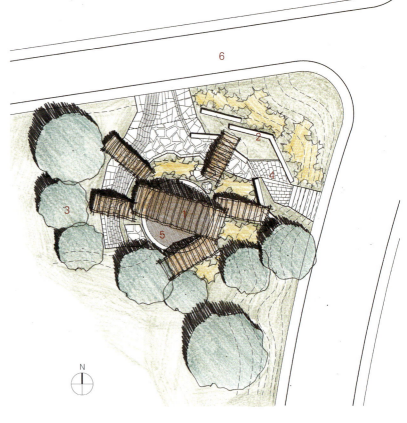

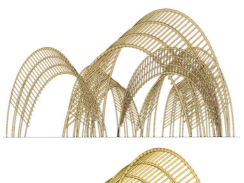

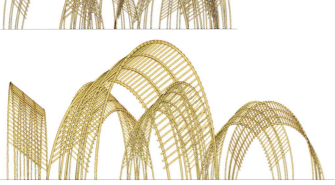

▲ 总平面图
Master Plan

1　竹编构筑物组群
　　Bamboo Structure Groups
2　景观小挡墙
　　Landscape Small Retaining Wall
3　樱花林
　　Cherry Blossom Grove
4　碎砖碎石铺地
　　Brick&Rubble paving
5　圆形舞台
　　The Circular Stage
6　入村道路
　　Road of the Village Entrance

▲ ▼ 入口竹编构架和场地　Entrance Bamboo Structures & Ground

05 景观 Landscape

村内景观节点　　Landscape Nodes in the Village

景观设计主要结合建筑改造，腾出部分街道空间，植入游览及活动空间，增加乡村景观的可观赏性，以及游客的参与性与体验感。

同时，随着城市发展，湖熟文化遗存在村内基本无处可寻。景观也挖掘再现了湖熟八景中的"凉台映月"与"孤灯夜照"景点，以再现古代湖熟文化中曾经繁华的胜迹。

主要节点有：钱家渡民宿服务中心环境、孙家桥游客服务中心环境、凉台映月及孤灯夜照。

Within the rural residential area, the landscape design is mainly combined with architectural renovation, freeing up part of the street space, implanting tourism and activity space, increasing the viewability of the rural landscape, along with the participation and experience of tourists.

At the same time, with the development of the city, the Hushu cultural heritage is basically nowhere to be found in the village. The landscape also reproduced two of the eight scenic spots of Hushu, in order to reproduce the past prosperous sights in the ancient culture.

The main nodes are: environment of Qianjiadu Homestay Service Center, environment of Sunjiaqiao Tourist Service Center, Moon-Viewing Terrace and night illumination pavilion.

◀ 村内活动场地　Village Activity Area

钱家渡民宿服务中心环境 Environment of Qianjiadu Homestay Service Center

钱家渡民宿服务中心作为游客主要的休憩建筑，其周边布局了相对开敞的广场空间。

广场铺地力求自然，质朴，采用村内拆旧所剩石材为材料，自然碎拼，同时利用干垒块石形成菜畦、种植池等小空间环境；同时，结合水上游线，在面水侧布置了停靠码头。

As the main resting building for tourists, the Qianjiadu Homestay Service Center is surrounded by relatively open square space.

The paving of the square strives to be natural and simple. Leftover stones from the demolition of the village are used with naturally fragment layout. At the same time, dry blocks are applied to form small space such as vegetable borders and planting ponds. A dock is placed on the side which faces the water, becoming a part of the tourist ship route.

▲ 总平面图
Master Plan

1 钱家渡民宿服务中心
Qianjiadu Homestay Service Center

2 中心小广场
Central Plaza

3 菜畦
Vegetable Garden

4 码头
Wharf

5 步行桥
Pedestrain Bridge

6 叠落石头花坛
Stone Laying Parterrel

7 现状大香樟
Present Camphor Tree

◀ 东侧景观 Landscape from East

05 景观　Landscape

▲ 民宿服务中心门前广场
　Entrance Plaza of the Homestay Service Center

▼ 民宿服务中心周边景观
　Surrounding Landscape of the Homestay Service Center

孙家桥游客服务中心环境 Environment of Sunjiaqiao Tourist Service Center

景观设计以连续的序列空间组织引导建筑入口空间。端头以"门头"为意向，点名村名。

沿途设计以竹篱笆和土石墙形成蜿蜒的线形空间，组织行进路线，同时分割和收放空间。

The landscape design guides the building entrance space with continuous sequential spatial organization. The image of "mentou" serves as the end of the route to point out the name of the village.

Along the road, the design uses bamboo fences and earth stone walls to form a serpentine linear space, organizing the route of travel by dividing and retracting the space and view at the same time.

◀ 总平面图
Master Plan

1 孙家桥游客服务中心
  Sunjiaqiao Tourist Service Center
2 中心小广场
  Center Small Square
3 次入口
  Secondary Entrance
4 篱笆与土石墙
  Fence&Earth–Stone Wall
5 雨水花园
  Rainwater Garden
6 入口牌坊
  Entrance Memorial Archway
7 入村道路
  Road of the Village Entrance
8 步行拱桥
  Walking Arch Bridge

▲ 雨水花园　Rainwater Garden

◀ 篱笆与步道　Fence & Footpath

凉台映月　Moon-Viewing Terrace

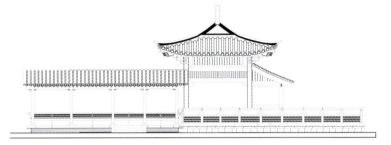

▲ 东立面　East Elevation

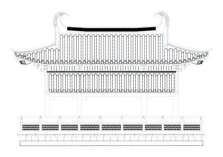

▲ 迎水立面　Elevation Facing the Water

05 景观　Landscape

孤灯夜照　Night Illumination Pavilion

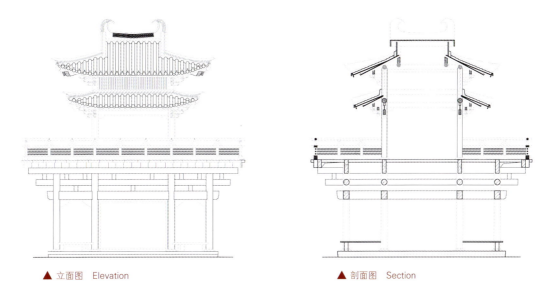

▲ 立面图　Elevation　　　　▲ 剖面图　Section

06 后续
Follow-up

生活：乡村居民　Living of Rural Residents

当地原住民在村庄转型发展中收入得到提升，主要通过三个途径实现：一是普通农民职业化，此举解决 50 岁以上村民就业 23 人，年均收入 5 万元；二是通过村企合作、资源发包，引导村民就业创业；三是社区组织了农技培训，提高了村民的思想境界和种养技能。

2019 年，钱家渡村开展各类文体活动 65 场，丰富了辖区内村民的精神文化需求，营造了和谐、文明、喜庆的节日氛围，增强了村民的凝聚力和向心力。面向原住村民多次开展包粽子、新年送福等节事活动和种植评比活动，提升了村民的满足感和获得感。

村民自愿成立了多个志愿服务队，配合国资平台承担村庄后期的运营维护工作。例如由老党员、老村长及一些热心公益的村民组成的夕阳红志愿者服务队，佩戴治安巡逻红袖章进行日常巡逻，化解矛盾，在钱家渡村建设期间，保障了工程建设的顺利推进。

The income of local aborigines has been improved in the transformation and development of the village, which is achieved in three main ways: first, the vocationalization of ordinary farmers, a move that solved the employment of 23 villagers over 50, with an average annual income of 50,000 yuan; second, through the cooperation of village enterprises and the issuance of resources, villagers are guided to employment and entrepreneurship; third, the community organized agricultural training, which improved the villagers' ideology and farming skills.

In 2019, Qianjiadu Village carried out 65 various cultural and sports activities, which enriched the spiritual and cultural needs of villagers in the district, enhanced the cohesion and centripetal force of villagers. For the indigenous villagers, many festive activities have been carried out to enhance the villagers' satisfaction and sense of gain.

Villagers set up several volunteer teams to cooperate with the state-owned platform to undertake the operation and maintenance of the village at a later stage. For example, by conducting daily patrols and resolving conflicts, the Sunset Red Volunteer Service Team ensures the construction progress of the project during the construction of the village.

06 后续 Follow-up

164-165 页部分照片由南京田园水韵建设开发有限公司提供

体验：城市游客 Experiencing of Urban Tourists

自2018年5月试运营开始，村庄特色风貌和活动吸引了大量游客前往。截至2019年12月，接待游客已超过30万人次。

乡村在建设中秉承着因地制宜的原则，延续原有生态肌理，没有大拆大建，运用了一些旧农具、老物件在村中成为独特的景观。例如篱笆围栏的设计，尽量运用本地的乡土材料，木质围栏、竹制篱笆以及渔网的使用很好地展现了乡土风情。

由普通民舍、废弃小学、废弃排涝站改造而成的水边民宿、水上餐厅和水岸清吧，在保留水乡特色的前提下，置入面向城市游客的新功能。高品质的空间和高水平的服务一改传统乡村农家乐的粗糙，满足当下城市游客的需求。

传承民俗和历史的水乡特色活动，为城市游客带来具有地域性的游览体验，重塑水乡生活方式。民俗活动传承乡村历史记忆，实现城乡同乐。

Since the trial operation began in May 2018, the village has attracted a large number of tourists. As of December 2019, more than 300,000 tourists have been received.

The construction of the village adheres to the principle of adapting measures to local conditions and continues the original ecological texture. There is no major demolition and construction, and some old farm tools and old objects are used to create a unique landscape in the village. The use of wooden fences, bamboo fences and fishing nets shows the local customs well.

The waterside homestays, restaurants and bars rebuilt from abandoned buildings are equipped with new infrastructure for urban tourists while retaining the characteristics of the water village. High quality spaces and services have changed the roughness of traditional rural farmhouses to meet the needs of current urban tourists.

The water village characteristic activities that inherit folk customs and history bring a regional tour experience to city tourists and reshape the water village lifestyle. Folklore activities inherit the historical memory of the village and realize the fun of urban and rural areas.

06 后续 Follow-up

166–167 页部分照片由南京田园水韵建设开发有限公司提供

运营：农业合作社　Operation with Agricultural Cooperatives

在钱家渡特色田园发展期间，和平社区大力扶持农民专业合作社。其中比较有规模的是以下两家：杨长根水稻种植专业合作社与南京润和水产养殖农地股份专业合作社。两家合作社共流转约600名村民的土地共计3700多亩，流转金额为700元每亩，其带动其他零散八九家大户，有1000多亩。总共占到我们社区总耕地面积（6128亩）的70%以上。

杨长根家庭农场，流转土地1400亩，固定用工9人，人均年收入4万元，解决本村年龄50岁以上的老年人就业难题，季节性用约60人；主要在尝试龙虾水稻混养，龙虾水稻混养大米定价大约为8元一斤。

南京润和合作社流转了土地及水面约2300亩，有25位工作人员，均为普通农民变职业农民，设立粮油种植、水产养殖和蔬菜种植三部分，有效帮助工作人员人均收入增加近万元。

During the development of Qianjiadu, Heping Community vigorously supported farmers' professional cooperatives. Among them, there are two models: Yang Changgen Rice Planting Professional Cooperative and Nanjing Runhe Aquaculture Farmland Cooperative. The two cooperatives transferred a total of more than 3,700 mu land for about 600 villagers. The transfer price was 700 yuan per mu, which led to other scattered large households with more than 1,000 mu. A total of more than 70% of the total arable land area (6128 mu) of our community is occupies.

Yang Changgen's family farm has 1,400 mu land in circulation, 9 permanent employees with an annual income of 40,000 yuan. It solves the employment problem of the elderly over 50 in the village. About 60 people are employed seasonally. The rice price of lobster and rice polyculture is about 8 yuan per 500 g.

Nanjing Runhe Cooperative has transferred more than 2,300 mu land and water surface, and has 25 staff members, all of whom are ordinary farmers turning into professional farmers. It mainly focuses on grain and oil planting, aquaculture and vegetable planting, which effectively helped the staff achieve income increase by nearly 10,000 yuan.

06 后续 Follow-up

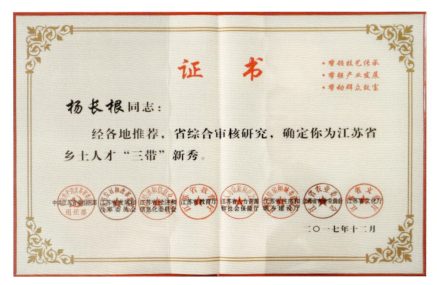

168-169页照片由南京市江宁区湖熟街道和平社区提供

运营：乡镇企业家及国资公司
Operation with Township Entrepreneurs and State-Owned Companies

钱家渡特色田园乡村由国资平台旅游产业集团田园水韵公司投资建设，并承担后期运营工作。

建设以来，钱家渡吸引了众多城镇企业主、高校毕业生返乡创业。现有91位高校毕业生就职于田园水韵公司，负责钱家渡村的日常经营维护。7位城镇企业主入驻钱家渡，主营民宿和餐饮。外出务工人员返乡创业66人，主要是原本没有就业渠道的周边村民，现从事保安、保洁、职业农民等工作。

实际运营中，钱家渡借助互联网，创新多种宣传和销售途径。钱家渡的电商服务站，就近在线上线下销售钱家渡的善米、橹韵等特色农产品，有效实现了农民的增收。"金陵水乡·钱家渡"微信公众号结合四季农时积极推送乡村各类活动，成为钱家渡对外宣传新平台。

Qianjiadu Village is invested and constructed by Tianyuanshuiyun Company of the State owned Assets Platform Tourism Industry Group, and the Company undertakes the subsequent operation.

Since its construction, Qianjiadu has attracted many urban business owners and college graduates to return home to start businesses. At present, 91 college graduates work in the Company, responsible for the daily operation and maintenance of Qianjiadu Village. Seven urban business owners settled in Qianjiadu, mainly engaging in homestay and catering. 66 migrant workers returned to their hometown to start businesses, mainly engaging in security, cleaning, and professional farmers at present.

Qianjiadu used the Internet to innovate a variety of publicity and sales channels. Qianjiadu's e-commerce service station sells its special agricultural products such as rice online and offline, effectively increasing farmers' income. "Jinling Water Town · Qianjiadu" WeChat public account actively promotes various activities in the countryside in conjunction with the four seasons of farming, and has become a new platform for Qianjiadu's external publicity.

06 后续　Follow-up

 金陵水乡钱家渡
金陵水乡·钱家渡，江宁田园乡村中部核心启动区，典型江南水乡，乘坐...
2位朋友关注

进入公众号　　不再关注

家庭农场
昨天 晚上6:38

× 家庭农场（一）
2020年07月13日　星期一　16:17:30

水乡游乐

170–171 页部分照片由南京田园水韵建设开发有限公司提供

管理：社区街道   Management by Community and Sub-district Office

钱家渡特色田园乡村建设过程中，村两委工作积极性高，村级带头人成立钱家渡领导小组，在 2018 年 5 月 1 日开始的试运营期间多次与田园水韵公司对接，确保正式运营。建设期间社区街道从选址到规划设计的参与，充分调动了村民的积极性。钱家渡的规划设计充分征求村民意见，发放 51 户调查问卷。

2016 年，钱家渡村集体收入是 17.8 万元，当年被列入南京市的市级经济薄弱村，通过特色田园乡村的发展，2019 年达到 420 万元，在经济发展方面获得显著成效。

钱家渡在建设到运营期间，湖熟社区发放了 45 份村民满意度调查表。村民对村庄的建设内容和成效都非常满意，对村庄的发展充满信心。

During the construction of Qianjiadu's characteristic rural village, the two village committees were highly motivated to work. The village leaders established the Qianjiadu Leading Group. During the trial operation period that began in May 1,2018, they have docked with Tianyuanshuiyun Company several times to ensure the opening. Villagers participated from site selection to planning and design during the construction period under the organization of the village leading group. Qianjiadu's planning and design fully solicited the opinions of villagers, and issued questionnaires to 51 households.

In 2016, the collective income of Qianjiadu Village was 178,000 yuan. It was listed as a municipal economically weak village in Nanjing that year. Through the development of characteristic rural villages, it reached 4.2 million yuan in 2019, which is remarkable results in economic development.

From the construction to the operation of Qianjiadu, Hushu Community issued 45 villagers' satisfaction surveys. The villagers were very satisfied with the content and effectiveness of the village's construction and were full of confidence in the future of the village.

06 后续 Follow-up

172-173 页照片由南京市江宁区湖熟街道和平社区提供

设计:建筑团队　Planning and Design by Professional Team

钱家渡特色田园乡村严格按照规划方案实施,由东南大学建筑学院王建国院士团队进行规划、建筑和景观的更新。

设计团队对钱家渡项目选址、项目改建、项目变更,甚至水系水生植物选择等方面都非常重视,在村庄建设期间多次亲临现场对钱家渡规划进行指导。

Qianjiadu's characteristic rural village was implemented in strict accordance with the planning plan. The team of Academician Wang Jianguo from the School of Architecture of Southeast University attached great importance to Qianjiadu project.

The design team payed full attention to site selection, building reconstruction, project changes, water system aquatic plants and other aspects by visiting the site many times throughout the whole construction period.

06 后续 Follow-up

设计：建筑团队　　Planning and Design by Professional Team

2018年，东南大学建筑学院团队以钱家渡规划建筑设计为内容的参赛作品"渡·田·居——城郊融合视角下的钱家渡乡村振兴"获学生组2018年"紫金奖·建筑及环境设计大赛"金奖、优秀作品奖一等奖、江苏省社科应用研究精品工程奖一等奖。

设计方案抓住了钱家渡村的主要特点，突出了该村田野环境下滨河渡口文化特色。重点把握三个方面的因素：渡——水岸码头的传统历史文化；田——乡间田野的农耕生态气息；居——主客共享的滨水良居环境。较好地挖掘了乡村中乡愁的记忆情怀和适宜的形态表达，使乡村既有文化传承发展，又突显当今生活气息。

In 2018, the team of the School of Architecture of Southeast University's entry "Ferry · Farmland · Residential—Qianjiadu Rural Revitalization from the Perspective of Urban and Suburban Integration" won the 5th "Zijin Award" of Architectural Design and Environmental Art Contest Gold Medal, First Prize of Excellent Works Award; First Prize of Jiangsu Province Social Science Applied Research Outstanding Project Award.

The design captures the main characteristics of Qianjiadu Village and highlights the cultural features of the riverside crossing in the village's environment. Focusing on three factors: crossing—the traditional historical culture of the waterfront wharf; field—the farming ecological atmosphere of the countryside; dwelling—the waterfront living environment shared by the host and guest. The design has well excavated the memories of homesickness in the countryside and suitable expressions, preserving the cultural inheritance and development while highlighting the atmosphere of today's life.

06 后续 Follow-up

项目负责人	王建国，朱渊
技术设计负责人	王晓俊，殷伟韬
规划局负责人员	胡传宏，王振友，李荣平
参与设计人员	
水边民宿：	乔炯辰
民宿服务中心：	奚涵宇
土地庙：	奚涵宇
乡村生活馆：	张皓翔
乡村书屋：	廖若微
水上餐厅：	奚涵宇
水岸清吧：	孔圣丹
钱家渡民舍修整：	张皓翔，宗袁月
景观设计：	钱筠，许若菲，邓慧叜，裴中岳，佘晶晶，钱雪飞，张杰
建筑施工图设计：	殷伟韬，盛吉，许立群
结构设计：	廖振
给排水设计：	韩治成
电气设计：	沈梦云
前期概念规划	南京城理人城市规划设计有限公司
摄影	王建国院士团队，侯博文
本书编撰人员	宗袁月，钱筠，罗梓馨，孔圣丹，罗文博